From reviews of *Judevine*, the play and the poems:

"Wrenchingly real, fiercely emotional and unexpectedly funny."
— *Chicago Sun Times*

"Budbill [writes] with rare honesty, affection, and grace — and with language so precise and descriptive you will know immediately you're soul-deep in something extraordinary."
— *Los Angeles Daily News*

"For twenty years, David Budbill has been writing about his small-town and rural Vermont neighbors — tree farm laborers, mechanics, junk ("antique") dealers, hard-scrabble farmers — some of the most direct and clear-eyed poems of the half-century, at least. Budbill's poems have the rhythmic life of the best of Jeffers and are as large-souled and democratic as Whitman. Although as full of New England salt as Frost's, they are far more compassionate, more Christian in the finest sense of the word. For Budbill's personae are the poor and oppressed, and he is as staunchly their advocate — an angry protester of the way weekenders and land speculators have displaced the people of northern Appalachia — as Sandburg ever was. He is emotional but not sentimental: his single greatest character, foul-mouthed Acadian laborer Antoine LaMotte, is as gross — and as vital — as Chaucer's Wife of Bath. Many are going to say *Judevine* is as good as Masters' *Spoon River Anthology*. Okay, but off the mark: *Judevine* may be better thought of as the book James Agee was ultimately too pious and too distanced from his subjects to write. *Judevine* is a great book."
— *Booklist*, "Editor's Choice" starred review

"Budbill writes with tremendous authority, high and low humor (some of this is very funny), and an unembarrassed passion for the community and individuals in it. Here is everything we are so often told is missing from contemporary poetry: it is rooted in the soil . . ., not the ego of the poet; it is magnanimous in scale and in spirit; it makes grand music of many voices — crying out to be read aloud. . . . Budbill lives by Camus' injunction in his Nobel prize speech: 'It's a part of a writer's duty to speak for those who cannot speak for themselves.'"
— *The Beloit Poetry Journal*

"David Budbill's . . . poetry is as accessible as a parking lot and plain as a pair of Levi's . . . [*Judevine*] is a labor of love not in the usual sense that the artist can be seen to love the labor he performs but because he can be seen to love the place and the people he's writing about."
— Thomas Disch, *Parnassus*

Budbill's is an important voice, part of the nascent movement to bring our view of New England's native poor from the long-vanished world of Ethan Frome to the likes of the Beans of Egypt, Maine. Essential . . .
— *Library Journal*

OTHER WORKS BY DAVID BUDBILL

POETRY

Moment to Moment: Poems of a Mountain Recluse
Why I Came to Judevine
From Down to the Village
The Chain Saw Dance
Barking Dog

PLAYS

Judevine: The Play in Three Acts
Two for Christmas
Little Acts of Kindness
Thingy World!
Judevine: The Play in Two Acts
A Pulp Cutters' Nativity
Knucklehead Rides Again
Mannequins' Demise

SHORT STORIES

Snowshoe Trek to Otter River

NOVELS

Bones on Black Spruce Mountain

CHILDREN'S BOOKS

Christmas Tree Farm

EDITED VOLUME

Danvis Tales: Selected Stories by Rowland Robinson

COMPACT DISK

*Zen Mountains—Zen Streets: A Duet for Poet and
Improvised Base* with William Parker (a 2-CD set)

JUDEVINE

DAVID BUDBILL

CHELSEA GREEN PUBLISHING COMPANY
White River Junction, Vermont
Totnes, England

for Lois and Nadine

03 02 01 00   2 3 4 5

Judevine was designed and typeset in Bembo by Kate Mueller/Chelsea Green Publishing Company.

Library of Congress Cataloging-in-Publication Data
Budbill, David.
    Judevine / David Budbill. — [New ed.]
      p.   cm.
    Includes index.
    ISBN 1-890132-22-5 (alk. paper)
    1. City and town life—Vermont—Poetry.   I. Title.
  PS3552.U346J83 1999
  811'.54—dc21   98–53059

Chelsea Green Publishing Company
P.O. Box 428
White River Junction, VT 05001
(800) 639-4099
www.chelseagreen.com

CONTENTS

PART III

PREFACE TO THE NEW EDITION

I started writing the Judevine poems in 1970. The earliest small collection, *The Chain Saw Dance*, first published by The Crow's Mark Press, appeared in 1977, and then was re-published by Countryman Press in 1983.

In 1980 the first staged reading of some of the poems, plus a reading of the poem/play *A Pulp Cutters' Nativity*, occurred at McCarter Theatre in Princeton, New Jersey.

In 1981, The Ark published the second collection of poems, *From Down to the Village*, and Countryman Press published *A Pulp Cutters' Nativity*.

In 1984, McCarter Theatre produced a fully mounted, early version of what would become *Judevine: A Play in Two Acts*. From this point forward both the play and the poems began to develop side by side, each influencing the other.

In 1987 White Pine Press brought out *Why I Came to Judevine*, yet another small book of Judevine poems, while the play moved around the country continuing to develop and expand.

The play's development culminated, or so I thought at the time, with a Mainstage production at American Conservatory Theatre in San Francisco in 1990.

In 1991 Chelsea Green published *Judevine*, the collected poems, and in 1992 *Judevine: A Play in Two Acts* was published. It seemed to me then that I was done with that part of my writing life, both on the page and on the stage.

I was wrong. The play continued to develop and expand, and in 1996 *Two for Christmas*—my translation of the medieval, English miracle play, *The Second Shepherd's Play*, plus a revised version of *A Pulp Cutters' Nativity*—received its first stage production.

Then in 1997 I put together yet another version: *Judevine: A Play in Three Acts*.

This new edition of *Judevine*, with many rewrites and numerous additions, is meant to bring the book of poems up to date with the continuing development of the play.

People ask me if I'm done writing the Judevine poems and working on the play, and I say, yes, definitely. I say I'm on to other things, which is true, yet I seem to return to this place and these people, as if it were a homeland, from time to time still, almost thirty years later.

ACKNOWLEDGMENTS

Grateful acknowledgment to the following magazines in which some of these poems first appeared: *Arachne, The Beloit Poetry Journal, Bleb/The Ark, Claymore, Common Sense, Country Journal, Format: Art and the World, The Great Circumpolar Bear Cult, The Greenfield Review, The Greensboro Review, Harvard Magazine, Jam-today, Longhouse, New Letters, North Coast Poetry, The Ocooch Mountain News, The Ohio Review, Organic Gardening and Farming, Poetry Now, Poets Who Sleep #10, Quest/79, The Road Apple Review, Rumors Dreams and Digressions, Seeds of Change, Tamarack, Truck, The Vermont Vanguard Press, The Vermont Peace Reader,* and *White Pine Journal.*

"Raymond and Ann" first appeared in *Harper's Magazine.*

"Why I Came to Judevine" first appeared in *The Ohio Review* under the title, "Man at the Breech: My Uncle Freddy."

Portions of this book were originally published as *The Chain Saw Dance* by The Crow's Mark Press in 1977 and subsequently by Countryman Press in 1983; and as *From Down to the Village* by The Ark in 1981; and as *A Pulp Cutters' Nativity* by The Countryman Press in 1981; and as *Why I Came to Judevine* by White Pine Press in 1987.

The quotation from Thomas Merton in "Going Places" is taken from his essay "The Sacred City" as it appears in *Ishi Means Man,* published by Unicorn Press, Inc. in 1976, and is used here with permission of the publisher.

The original settler's narrative in "Journey for the North" is from a memoir published by Seth Hubbell in the 1884 edition of *Child's Gazetteer of Orleans and Lamoille Counties, Vermont.* I have altered and adapted what Seth Hubbell wrote to my own purposes, feeling no constraints to be faithful to anything but the spirit of the man and his story.

I want to acknowledge and thank Michael Moore, my editor at Chelsea Green and my friend, with whom I have wrestled as Jacob wrestled with the Angel.

I want also to acknowledge here the good counsel and friendship of Donald Hall, Geoffrey Gardner, John Haines, and three others, now dead, Millen Brand, George Dennison, and Joel Oppenheimer, whose encouragement and support over the past thirty years has seen me through many a dark time.

An especial note of thanks goes to two fellow poets and longtime friends who have read and reread this book in its many manifestations and who have given me support and counsel over many years: Howard Nelson, whose friendship and encouragement over the past twenty years have been indispensable and greatly welcome, and Hayden Carruth, who for thirty years, since before these poems began, has been an encouraging mentor, hawkeyed critic, and steadfast friend.

Finally, I want to acknowledge here my gratitude and debt to the many actors and directors in theaters all over America who have worked on the various productions of *Judevine* and the other plays, which are based on this collection. Through their enthusiastic portrayals of these characters and from their improvisations, I have gained much.

And, wel I woot, as ye goon by the weye,
Ye shapen yow to talen and to playe;
For trewely confort ne myrthe is noon
To ride by the weye doumb as a stoon;
And therefore wol I maken yow disport,
As I seyde erst, and doon yow som confort. . . .

And, for to make yow the moore mury,
I wol myselven gladly with yow ride
Right at myn owene cost, and be youre gide.

Geoffrey Chaucer
The Canterbury Tales

PART I

HERMIE

Hermie Newcome lived in a bread truck on the edge
of Bear Swamp.
The bread truck is still there
with a spruce tree through the roof and the remains
of his last pig pen.
He had a bunk up front where the seats used to be
so in the morning he could wake up and look out
the windshield at the day.
There was a little wood stove in the back.
Hermie brought the stove wood in
through the rear doors so he wouldn't have to
lug it through his bedroom.
There was a table and a chair
and some crates for cupboards.
It was always neat in there.
It was a good place and cozy.
Hermie didn't need anything big as a bus.

His woman, Florence, was an Indian from New York.
Before he lived in the bread truck, they had a shack
next to the Dunn Hill cemetery and before that
they lived on Hermie's family place
on the Aiken Pond road up from the schoolhouse
where I used to live.
But one night while they were still at the home place,
Hermie got pissed at something, nobody knows what,
and flew into a rage, which he did about twice a week,
but this time went too far and lit both house and barn
and watched them burn.
When the neighbors came Hermie was out in the snow,
in the dooryard stomping and screaming:
Burn! Goddamnit!
Burn! you wuthless place.
You never was no goddamn good!

Nobody could ever be quite sure when Hermie was drunk.
He acted crazy all the time.
There's nothing left of the Newcome place now,
only the spring box. Those tamarack boards
will last forever.

Then they moved over to the shack by the cemetery.
Hermie liked it there,
said it was the first place he ever lived
where he had decent neighbors.

Antoine tells about going past there on a Saturday night
and seeing
Hermie and Florence dancing with the chain saw going
in the middle of the floor.
Hermie and Florence'd get drunk,
then Hermie would adjust the carburetor on the saw
so it would run too rich
so it would sputter, bounce with a rhythm
worthy of a good musician.
Then they'd sing and dance
to the music of the saw.

Hermie could cut pulp like a son of a bitch;
he could bull and jam when he wanted to,
but that wasn't very often.
Everybody said he was worthless.
Hiram still says
his mother should of knocked him in the head when he was born
and spent the money on some grain to raise a pig.

Hermie never did anybody any harm;
in fact the night he burnt the home place
he was sure to get Florence and the cats out
before he struck the match.

He burnt the cemetery place too.
That's when Florence left him, went back
to the reservation or to Morrisville.
I don't know where.

Then he moved alone into the bread truck in the swamp.
Hermie spent his life looking for the perfect place.
That's what all those fires were about.
And in the end he found that place.
The bread truck wouldn't burn.

OLD MAN PIKE

Old man Pike was a sawyer at the mill
in Craftsbury.
He lived just down the road from here.
Every morning he walked six miles through the woods
over Dunn Hill saddle while the sun rose.
He took dinner and supper in the village,
then walked home across the mountain in the dark.
Sally Tatro who used to live on my place
would hear him coming through the night, singing.
Sometimes he'd stop to gossip
but mostly she only saw him stride by the window
and disappear.

The old man could have stayed at home,
milked cows, like everybody else,
but he needed an excuse to go and come
through the mountains, every day,
all his life, alone.

Old man Pike didn't believe in the local religion of work,
but out of deference, to his neighbors maybe,

he bowed to it,
placed its dullness at the center of his life,
but he was always sure, because of his excuse,
to wrap it at the edges of his days
in the dark and solitary amblings of his pleasure.

ANSON

Anson was born on the place next door, half a mile away.

About ten years ago the university took part of the Boynton place
    for taxes.
(The university, by the way, has been delinquent on the taxes ever
    since.)
Not long after that the Boyntons sold out, but Anson came back a
    few years ago
with a French wife and two sons to farm his home.
He rented from the owner, a chiropractor in California.
Anson sold out last spring.
The bank wouldn't loan him money for machinery
because he didn't own the place and because
the chiropractor wouldn't give him a long-term lease.

Anson's gone.
Kicked off the place he was born on
by somebody he never met.

They were good neighbors. My boy and their boys
played together, rode their bikes up and down the road,
built forts in the woods, fished for trout in the brook,
gave each other courage to make it through a day at school.

Anson spread shit on our garden free of charge,
helped me draw my wood, used to take all three boys

6

on a sleigh behind his snow machine.
Marie took the boys to Morrisville to the movies.
She was pretty and alive. It was fun
to watch her move across a room.
We never visited all that much but they were good neighbors.

Anson busted his ass over there. It was his home
even if he did have to rent it. He busted his ass
and for nothing.

Everybody says the Boynton place is jinxed,
says nobody can make a go of it over there.
Anson could have if he'd had a break.
It's not the farm that's jinxed; it's farming.
Grain goes up, milk goes down.
The U.S. secretary of agriculture has deliberately
conspired against the family farm.
The name of the game in Washington is agribusiness,
huge consolidated farms big as Continental Can.
Down there they want the family farm to die.
They want fewer and fewer people
to have more and more money.

This is not my fantasy.
The Associated Press reported last week
that the secretary of agriculture admitted during a senate hearing
that he thought the family farm should be "phased out."

Here's the secretary again: "Farming isn't a way of life.
It's a way to make a living."
God forbid somebody should see his life and living
as the same thing. What are these idiot neighbors of mine
doing anyway thinking they should love their work?
Don't they know the end of work is money?

Listen, this isn't an issue doesn't concern you.

This issue is the death knell
for what little anarchistic independence is left.
It is oligarchy's fanfare,
and the band plays louder every day.

Every summer Anson had a window box of flowers
near the milk house door
and every morning after chores
he watered them and then
with the thumb and forefinger of his calloused hand
he gently, gently plucked
the dying blossoms.

As I was saying, last May, on a Saturday, Anson and Marie
sold out. It was a good day.
Anson's prayers were answered.
He'd asked God not to let it rain.
As the sun came up Norman Pelletier—
the auctioneer—
drove down Route 15 and up over the hill
to here and told Marie
to have an hour's worth of junk
to get the people started.

By ten o'clock trucks lined both sides the road
either way from their house half a mile to ours
and that far the other way too.
It was a farmer's auction, too early in the year
for summer people hunting antiques.
There weren't any antiques anyway.
Marie moved around the crowd forcing a smile and waving
like a maître d' serving up her life.

There was soda and hot dogs
and kids running around screaming, excited by the crowd.
Edith cried. So did Marie. Anson wanted to but didn't.

The farmers stood around and bid, raising a hand quietly,
nodding a head.
But there weren't any jokes.
They knew they were playing bit parts in a movie
about their own deaths.

At the end of the day
Anson had taken in thirty-seven thousand dollars
and all that in just machinery and stock.
Everybody said he done real good, *real* good.
But it wasn't good enough.

Anson's working as a mechanic in Burlington now.
He makes a hundred ten dollars a week for his family of four.
They've got a trailer in a trailer park.
We saw them a couple of months ago.
They said they missed it up here on the hill.

BILL

The Pikes have come a long way down
since the old man walked to Craftsbury
every day all his life to saw boards.
There's only Bill and Arnie left as far as I know
and both of them make only enough to stay drunk.

About five years ago one night in January
I dug Bill out of a snowbank.
It was two in the morning and thirty below.
He'd driven off the road where it crosses Bear Swamp.
He was dead drunk.
In fact, when I waded through the snow to his car
I thought he *was* dead,
and he would have been by morning,

of cold or carbon monoxide,
if I or someone hadn't come along.
The headlights were on and the radio, and Bill
slumped across the wheel with the motor running.
I banged on the door, opened it,
Bill rolled out, head first, into the snow, like a corpse.
I drug him to my car.
As the snow on his face melted, he woke up a little.
Probably he'd been to Cole's Pond Bottle Club.
It was Saturday night.

I shook him, asked him where he wanted to go.
All he did was point toward the village.
I knew when we got to Judevine he'd point to Hardwick,
then Danville, Newport, Derby, Eden,
on and on like that for days
while I drove around the ass end of the state and he sobered up,
which would be some time since
he brought the Bud with him.
But the bastard pointed me to Arnie's place
without the slightest error.

I think blind drunks have homing devices, like the ones in geese,
pickled in their livers.
They don't need to see, only point.
They know where home is.

Arnie was still up, drunk too.
I got him to come out and the two of us drug Bill up
over the rotten porch steps
and into a garbage can of empties.
We made such a racket getting him across the porch and into the
   house that the blue tick out back started howling.
We dumped him on the living room linoleum and I left.
Nobody said thank-you or good-bye.
In fact, in the years since nobody has ever mentioned the incident,

except once down at the garage Bill said "'lo" to me
and in his eyes there was the look of recognition.

We bought a pig from Bill one spring.
When I went into his rusty trailer to pay him
the place smelled like baby shit and kerosene.

The railroad's started up again
and Bill's got his old job back
when he's sober.
He still raises pigs I guess although I don't know
since even though his place is only a few miles from here
I haven't been past there in years.

I still see him now and then working on the tracks
or buying beer at the garage
but we never speak.

We don't know each other.

ANTOINE

Spring. 1970.
My first day as a laborer on a Christmas tree farm.
I pulled my pickup to the side of the road,
hopped over a drainage ditch running full
and started up a slope toward a man
standing about a quarter mile away.
Even now, the first of May,
the woods still stood in better than a foot of rotten snow,
but here where the earth tilted south the ground was bare.
Above the grays and browns of last year's matted grass
the young Christmas trees seemed iridescent
in the morning sun.

Antoine stood motionless, watching me come up the hill.

You da new mans? Taut you was. Mike said you
was caumin'. I'm Antoine LaMotte! I live alone
ina trailer up on Aiken Pond. Shitagoddamn!
good to be in da sun again!

He offered me a cigarette and lit us both.

Antoine is a small man, five two or three.
About his cheeks there is that unmistakable alcoholic sheen.
His neck moves in deepening shades of red toward the back until
between his hair line and his collar
it is the color of wild strawberries.
His hair is thin but black and his dark eyes dance
when he talks, which he does incessantly.
His whole body moves with the rhythm of his words;
his hands flutter in front of him as if they were
dancing to the music of his speech.
He walks like a duck.
He bangs around the house of his body like a baby.
He is small, feather light, delicate and infinitely tender.

We stood for a long time smoking, looking out
over the mountains.

Wall! you mus' be crazy fauckin' basterd take
a job like dis! Bull an' jam like da rest of us
for two an' a korter an'our. You crazy as me!
By Chris' an' Saint Teresa don't you say I didn't
warn you. Before you're done, your tongue hang out,
touchhole hang daown, you pull an' tug 'till
you cast your wid'ers. Your mamma
roll over in 'er grave, cry out,
Oh! by Jesus, how I fail you as a mudder!
When you go home tonight your little wimens

she gonna haf 'ta take a rain check.
She gonna hate you tonight!
An' you gonna start to hate dese friggin' trees.
You gonna wish your mudder be a baby girl!

Wall, what else is dere ta do? No goddamn work
'raound here anymore. Guess you know dat
else you weren't be daum enough to be 'ere.
Naow! no work. No work atall.
Can't mi'k caows anymore.
I yanked does titties, shauveled dat shit, all my life, den
dey caum an' say I gots to haf' a bulk tank,
an' I can't keep a pig in da barn, an' I godda wash
my han's in dis and my feets in dat, julluk I be
some kinda brain sergen or sut'in.'
So I say shit to dat an' haf a nauction
an' I be glad to git done too, fer 'bout a day.
Den I begin dreamin' 'bout dem caows and haf' a version.
I could see 'em standin' in der stalls. My little
girlfriends, an' I wander 'raound dat empty barn
an' oh! by Jesus, I was sick in my heart!
Nat'in' to do wi' my days. Naut'in'.
So I caum crawlin' over here, work out,
be saumbody else's slave, 'steada my own,
an' now I sleep in one of dem friggin' ice boxes
all to myself an' watch saum downcountry saumbody
tear daown my house an' barn what I was born in, shit!
Nat'in' ta do 'raound here nomore.

All da quarries over to Buffalo Mountain gone.
Stun sheds in Hardwick all fallin' daown.
Nat'in' over dere but rats and crazy ol' Artie Mezey
hidin' in da sheds inside an ol' car drinkin'
blackberry brandy an' waitin' for saum little boys
to caum along. Chris'! da whole goddamn taown
just fallin' in da reever. Ah! when I was a boy

it weren't dat way. Dey was mills an' bars.
T'irty-tew bars in dat little place!
Haf' good times der too, wall I guess!
Good whorehouse too. I used to go confession
over to da church on Friday afternoon
den step across da street take in a little matinee.
Da church still der, but da whorehouse she ain't.

When da sheds close daown dat town shrivel
like a moldy squash. Nat'in' left.
On'y saum ol' wop cudders, ones still livin',
what can't go out winners 'cause a da air, stayin' ta home
coughin' out der lungs. Ah! wadda you care!

There was an embarrassed silence.
Then he went on.

Wall, here we be, ain't we? No more sittin'
by da stof 'til Doc say you be done.
Shitagoddamn, goddamnashit, dis da right place to be
caum spring, bull an' jam 'raound here outin da sun
t'in yer blood. Don't need no tonic here, shitacat'sass naow!
Ol' Doc give us a tonic. Couple weeks a walkin'
twenty miles a day spredin' dis fauckin' fert'lizer
an' your blood'll be runnin' good. Rock. Jus' rock
ya know. Dat's what we're spreddin' all day long;
15-10-10 an' wha's da odder sistyfife? Rock!
'nert 'greedients is what dey try to tell you,
but don't you beliefit, Mister Man, it's rock,
peacestone, from da mine, groun' up fine. Geewiss,
Geewiss Christ! ya'd t'ink a man a forty-five do saumt'in' sides
sprinkle rock onto baby trees. Hell, comeon.
I'llgetjabucket.

We set off down the hill toward a tractor and a wagon
piled with eighty-pound bags of Old Fox fertilizer.

14

What you really do, David? Dat's your name, ain't it? David?
I know somebody like the likes a you ain't gonna spend his en-tire
life makin' love to dese friggin' trees!
What's really why you be here on dis eart'?

I was afraid you'd ask.

Dat bad, eh?

Yes.

Wall, you can go ahead an' tell me, 'cause I known plenty
   criminal in my day,
an' I know how to keep my moud broken-down
an' ou'da order when I haf' to. Some day when we got more time
an' less money, I'll tell you what it be like araound dese parts
back in da Prohibition days! Den you see how not much
you could be could be so bad compared to den!
What you really do?

I'm a . . . writer. I'm . . . a poet.

What's dat you say?

I am a poet. I write poetry.

Shitacat'sass naow! You do? You be?
Oh, goddamnit to shit, I am a proud man to meet you!
Oh, my mudder in heaven look down on me!
I be workin' wid a poet! A *man* what writes poetry!
Fuck me! Next what we gonna see araound dese parts!
Ah, David, we gonna haf' a good time togedder!

An' don't you worry none. Your secret safe wid me!
Why, when I was a boy back in dat Prohibition day
dere was diamond ring bury in da dirt beneat' da porch

15

and submachine gun under da hay in da barn,
an' I never knew a t'ing about dem.
Ah, goddamnit to shit, I like poetry!

When I first knew Antoine he drank a lot,
a six-pack for breakfast on the way to work,
then another couple during the day.
I'm sure he drank himself to sleep.
But he never missed work and he never drank anything
but beer. He swore that if you drank only beer
you'd never become an alcoholic.

I'm no alacholic. Not like Uncle Clyde. He got
alacholic tumor big as a cabbage in his stomach.
Got to feed it brandy every day.
Me, I ain't nat'in' but a goddamn drunk.
Alacholism for da multitude millionaire. Politicians.
Poor fauckin' basterds da likes a me jus' goddamn drunks.

David, you like politics? I watch dat news
'baout ever' night. Watch dem crazy basterds
jomp araound. Goddamn multitude millionaires.
Gangsters. Any of 'em wort a turd get a bullet
in da head. All dem Kennedys and dat Martin
Lutter King. Oh Jesus! how I love dat man!
He like me, radder be a lover dan a fi'der.
See how far it got 'im! Naow! white man da biggest basterd
whatever live. Steal da country from da Indian
den make da nigger do da work!

Like me, da white nigger of da nord.

Wall, people's mean
all over. Up here it's skinhead 'gainst da frog.
I know what dey call me an' I don' care.
Let 'em call me what dey want if dat's da way

dey get der pleasure. Elwin tol' me what Alfreda said
'baout me not havin' no more brains 'an a frog's got feadders.
Wall, she got peacesoup in her veins too! Hell, wadda I care.
Nigger a da nord, dat's me, an' I don' care.
Poof! I know plenty. I just can' t'ink of it.
I see frogs she never wid hands big as hams,
once I even seen a snake wid legs up on Stannard Mountain,
but shit if I ever see a frog wid feadders.
Jus' 'cause she marry a skinhead drunk she t'ink herself
better 'an her gra'ma. She eat dem legs too.
Hell to her! You get yourself a bran sack full, skin 'em easy,
roll 'em flour, salt, pepper, fry 'em quick,
haf' a couple beers and, by Jesus, Mister, you got sut'in' good.

Then Antoine met Shirley.
They lived together in a trailer
up in Collinsville with her two boys.
About a month after all of us knew what was going on,
Antoine finally said:

David! got me a wimens! Workin' out, too. Workin' out good.
Two-hunnert-t'irty poun' and not an ounce a fat.
Caum up here from Joisey. Dat's how she say it.
Dat's how she talk.

She say, Hoi, Antoine, moi name's Shoiley. Oi just moved up heah
from New Joisey.
Would you boi any chance happen to have a glass
of wudder? Shitacat'sass, ain't dat funny?
Ah! it make me laugh da way she talk.

She is a good wimens.
I'd marry her tomorrow if it weren't we loose da welfare,
an' her wid dem two outlaw boys.
My rockin' chair money ain't enauf. Was for me,
get me tru da winner, but ain't for four a us.

If we be only two, be okay, but she got dem bad actin' saverges.
Shitagoddamn, if we be only two . . .
Wall, better'n livin' to myself in dat trailer
wi' nathin' but my goddamn dog.

It lasted about a year.
Then Shirley left, went down to a place in Barre.

David, she lef' me. Walk right aout. Poof!
I back in dat trailer wi' dat friggin' dog.
Only frien' I got. Two friggin' dogs.
Alone again. Just like dat goddamn Hermie.
Ah! goddamnit to shit, what's da use!
Piss on dat fire. Let's go drink saum beer.
Comeon, David, drink beer wid me.
Let's go drink saum beer.

I didn't go and I've been sorry ever since.
Antoine began missing more and more work until he was
   showing up about once a week.
That's when Bert fired him.

About a month after Antoine got fired he came over to my place
one Saturday afternoon. He was filthy. His eyes were beets.
He hadn't shaved in weeks.
He had a quart of Schaefer in his hand.

Dawyd, how yew be? Ah ain't tu good. Fawk,
Ah'm 'cinegratin', Dawyd. Caumin' apart tew pieces.
Ah doan know what Ah'm gonna dew. Ah didn't know ah luf
dat wimens so. Ah didn't know it. Mah mamma she be right.
Ah Christ, Ah wish to hell she still be a baby girl.

I didn't see Antoine for another couple months.
Then, again on a Saturday afternoon, he showed up,
clean clothes and shaven. He looked like his old self,

only better.

David! shitacat'sass, we back togedder!
Naow you better sid daown.
Dis gonna get you in da stomach,
right between da shoulder blades.

David, I gonna be a fadder!
By Christ, I never taut it caum to be.
Oh, my mamma be so pleased. She die t'inkin'
she fails me as a mudder, t'ink I gonna end my days
a smelly bach'er drunk. Dah last time midnight
New Year's Eve I caum in kneel at my fadder,
da year he die, I be turdy den, an get da blessin'
when he puts his han' on my head an' say da words
I know he a'mos' cry 'cause he know he iss dyin' and he know
I spen' my days yankin' my tool an' spillin' my seed.

Now dat little wimens got me growin' in 'er an',
Oh by Jesus, I be happy as a puppy to da road!
Oh! I wish to hell I could marry her!
She caum home from docter, sit daown a' table,
tell me, we bod' cry all afternoon, be so happy.
Next day I go to docter's say you help me naow,
I can' be drunk no more, I'm gonna be a fadder.
He say I be alacholic, I say Naow! how dat be!
I taut nobody be alacholic what drink only beer.
Dat's why I never drink dat hard stuff. He say, You are.
I didn't know it! Shitagoddamn, all dah years me t'ink
I nat'in' but a goddamn drunk I be high class alacholic
julluk da president!

He say I quit or I never see my baby grow,
and by Jesus dat t'ree week ago an' I ain't pull a ring since.
An' I ain't gonna to needer. We gonna name 'im . . . Pierre.
And if he be a girl, Michelle. Shitagoddamn, David,

naow I be like you book writers, I got my head
in da cloud, no more on da graoun' dan da moon,
an' Doc gimme my job back too. I tol' 'im
I got my reason to work naow. Fauck me!
I'll pick bluebird shit off da White Cliffs of Dover
if I haf' to.

Shirley had the baby and Antoine stomped around
like a bandy rooster.
Then it was spring again.

Graoun's a bullin', David. Time to plant da seed.
You got to make your wedder. Got to do it naow.
Just da right time. It's mudder nature. Like a wimens.
You be like me last year, cabbage an' tomato
gone to hell but I get a sidehill a patada
an' a baby girl. Dis year Poppa gonna plow
da whole goddamn state for his gardin!

Oh Jesus, I a'mos' forgot, dat hippie girl live up da road
caum over see da baby. She lean over coo,
her titties hangin' daown loose so big
dey weren't fid a sap bugit,
an' I see her pussy too stickin' out her pants
big as a witches broom. Bah gosh, David! how I wish
I be dat little baby!
Hell, an ol' buck got a stiff horn an' I ain't be done yet!

Shit, David, we got to get unmarried from dese goddamn trees!
I'm sick of it! I'm goin' home. Two o'clock an' I don't care.
I'm goin' to da matinee. I be!
I got to see dat wimens and my little baby.

You tell Doc I ain't functionatin' right today.
Tell 'im . . . I be back tamarra!

ARNIE

Arnie and I harvested Christmas trees three falls together.
Arnie is emaciated and always dirty.
He shaves only on Saturday nights
before he goes to the bottle club.
His face is more wretched than any I have ever seen.
All I remember about those falls together
is how much Arnie knew about the Second World War
and how his nose dripped.
He'd stand in the snow and shiver like a popple leaf
and his nose would drip.
He never bothered to wipe it
except maybe two or three times a day
he'd sop it gently
with the back of the glove on his right hand.
He had a filthy, ragged, black-and-green Johnson Woolen Mills
    jacket he wore summer and winter.
He stole it from the Mount Mansfield Company
when he worked there on the lifts, which is okay with me
since those in Stowe steal more from the likes of Arnie
than the likes of Arnie could ever imagine stealing from them.

Don't get me wrong. Arnie's no saint.
No proletarian archetype.
He's always in court.
He's a bad actor and everybody knows it.
But if we're going to discuss gangsters,
let's talk about the big time.

About Stowe, ski capital of the East, Stowe:
stolen from and supported by the state of Vermont.
The beautiful people's island plunked down
in the middle of the filth and loneliness
that stretches from Maine to Georgia, from top to bottom,
all the way down the Appalachian chain.

Let's talk about the thousands of farms gone under
so nice folks, like you, can have a place to lie around.
About a state of native slaves hanging around all winter
living off unemployment and welfare
waiting for the summer rich so they can mow a lawn
or paint a house for two and a quarter an hour.

Let's talk about the Vermont Development Department
and the "Beckoning Country," about their photographs
in *The New York Times* of white houses, red barns,
dirt roads and pretty cows, about why they don't take pictures
of Arnie's house or East Judevine or Hardwick or Island Pond
or a hundred other wretched towns. About why they don't
take pictures of kids with body lice or pictures of old ladies
who freeze to death in their beds. Let's talk about why
the legislators let their neighbors rot while they suck up
to those with money from Boston and New York, about how
four times a year *Vermont Life* sells a slick, full-color tumble
down the dreamy pit of nostalgia where,
for just two dollars a throw, you can sit wreathed
in an imaginary past.

Let's talk about the guy from Greenwich, Connecticut
with five thousand dollars worth of skis on his car
going down the road past Arnie Pike who makes
five thousand dollars a year.

I remember one day—in the fall, I think. It was warm
and we'd eaten lunch and were lying around with our boots off
talking about everything and laughing
and somehow I said—because I am who I am:
Life's really good, most of the time.
Something like that anyway.
And Arnie began shaking his head slowly and his eyes
got sad and: Naw, he said,
Naw. Not fer me.

Most athe time it ain't.
Then Arnie raised his head quick,
or as quick as slow Arnie could,
and his face had been transformed.
It was ghoulish, terrifying, as if the gates of hell
had tried to swallow him and he had got away.
Then he bared his rotten teeth and said, slow,
with a grin, while his nose dripped:
But ah'll survive.

Arnie and the other East Judevine uglies will survive,
in spite of the Mountain Company. They will survive
hidden away from downcountry skiers and the big money.
They will survive, wretchedly, but they will survive.
And when everybody thinks the gene pool has withered
to a ski bum and his après-ski bunny, then,
unknown to everyone who's supposed to know,
the ways of staying alive will still be known
by a few outlaws living in shacks
along the banks of the Wild Branch.

I was at Arnie's place just once after I took Bill there that night.
It was only a week before Arnie burnt out.
He always said he never bothered with fuses.
Pennies was just as good and cheaper.
Then he'd laugh and show his ugly teeth.
His place smelled like kerosene.
Nobody ever did know exactly why he burnt out,
but Arnie's no Hermie Newcome. He's too timid.
He didn't light it.
It was either the pot burner or the pennies.
Arnie survived.

It was the time I'm talking about when I was there
drinking beer at Arnie's place that he told me, and this
after knowing him five years, that he always had a doe

down cellar—always—year round:
I don't care nathin' fer the warden. He's afraid
ta caum up here. When Sam Raymond was around
he'd turn away.
Hell, he was an outlaw hisself.
That's why they made 'im warden.

Arnie went down to Massachusetts for a couple of years
to work in a shoe factory.
I guess he made pretty good money,
but he couldn't stand it down there.

One fall we were cutting trees up on Elmore Mountain
when color was still in the hills.
It was a clear day and we were up toward the top of the lot
looking out over the Lamoille valley at Eden Mountain
about thirty miles away.
That's when Arnie, Arnie the Wretched, the Ugly, the Stupid,
the Drunk, the Outlaw, the Poor—
that's when Arnie said:

Lookit 'at. 'At's why I live here.

And we looked across the ancient green and brown
and red and yellow mountains and the sky was blue
and some fleecy clouds and an osprey hunted the Lamoille
and we stood there while Arnie's nose dripped
and listened to the wind slip through the spruce trees.

✦ ✦ ✦

ANTOINE AND I GO FISHING

Saints an' me! I quit!

Look at what we live wid: Bert
an' he sayin' someday he iss gonna catch me workin'
when he come out here in da puckerbrush in his bat'room slipper
an' peek araoun' to spy on us. Wall, someday he might be,
but, by Jesus Christ, David, let's don't let it be today!

You know—you pro'bly don't—we been workin'
in dis lot all summer and up dis loggin' road
less'n half a mile is a pond what's full of trout,
I mean, Mister, full. I been t'inkin' on it all dis summer
an' today's da day we go up dere an' get our supper.

Poachin' and jackin' ain't too much for me;
I don't go sugarin' da way ol' Elwin use' to
wid a tank in back da trunk and gadder after dark
roadside buckets offin saumbody else's trees.
Dat's narrow.
Makin' sugar is too much work for dat!

But dese trout here naow just up da hill
is a differ'nt matter entirely since all Doc done
was drop a few into dat place when he built da t'ing.
Da fishes did da rest. So da way I see it
dey ain't no more his 'an anybody else's since da ones
he bought be caught or died long time ago,
an' what's left is only fishes what belong each odder
or demselves or to dem what hooks 'em
like da likes a you an' me.

Now how dat be? You t'ink I cipher good enough
get us up dere?

Oh, you don't have to worry none 'bout him caumin'.
I know Doc, know 'im well; he'd shoot us
just like he do his gramma. Nice fella, him.

Comeon, David, I bring you pole, put two in da trunk
dis mornin'. You scratch araound, get some worm,
I get da 'quip'ment an' we go.

I did as I was told and we were gone
up the hill into the shade of trees
and to the pond. In fifteen minutes
we had half a dozen of the nicest brook trout
I have ever seen.

Then Antoine startled:
Ho! Hear dat! Come on!
It's him, or Bert.
One shoot, d'odder fire.

Six trout flapping from an alder stick.
Two men run and stumble, giggle,
through the woods
back to the car.

Antoine hid the poles and fish inside his trunk
and we listened to a log truck
grinding down the hill toward the village:

Wall, six be da poacher's limit anyway.

WHY I CAME TO JUDEVINE

I

Cleveland. 1953.

Gertrude and Freddy, my aunt and uncle, live on the East Side,
    Alhambra Street, an Italian neighborhood.

Freddy's last name was Modine.

He ran a metal lathe at Picker X-Ray.

A good job; he didn't have to go outside and therefore had work
    in any weather, and he didn't have to lift or bend,

and the union scale was good or better than anything he had ever
    known before.

Alhambra Street was trying hard in 1953 to raise itself above its
    past.

Everyone washed and waxed his car at least once a week,

kept a postage stamp lawn of creeping bent, smoother, greener,
    more dense than any golf green in existence.

And Alhambra Street was trying hard to do away with street life.

Standing and drinking in the open was not a part of its vision of
    the future. People stayed inside, to themselves,

watched their new TV's, just like the people in the suburbs.

Going there may have been impossible, but acting like it was not.

But on summer evenings the old ways came back.

Maybe it was just the city heat, no breeze, or maybe it was
    remorse for such total abjuration of the past.

Whatever it was, it drew them out onto the porches.

Two porches to every house, one up, one down, what we called a
    "double house"—a house on top of a house.

Because of the climb the upper house was rented cheaper, but on
    summer nights, when the porches filled,

it was the better place to be.

You could lean on the railing and command the street.

On those summer evenings the men came home from the
    factories in their shiny Fords and Chevys,
squeezed them into narrow drives between the houses, climbed
    the stairs, drank their beer, ate their garlic and sausages,
then left the television dark and went onto the porches.

They sat on gliders, smoked and rocked;
or put themselves backward into straight-backed chairs, folded
    their arms over the tops,
and stared blankly into the street.
Then, slowly, the shouting from porch to porch, back and forth,
    began,
about how if that nigger Larry Doby struck out one more time
    they'd kill the bastard.
And in their hearts they were angry, jealous, and resentful that a
    black man, so handsome, smooth, and famous,
could be the subject of their voices.

Then the women, the fat women, having done the dishes, also
    came onto the porches
and sat on the gliders and also rocked, their hands folded gently
    across their abdomens,
laid gently like little balls of dough on their damp aprons.
Or they stood, the outside heel of each wrist propped on their
    hips, fingers dangling.

After the women settled themselves, the men would rise,
as if unnerved by the presence of their wives,
lean over the railing and stare, or pace a bit across the porch
in their white socks, their ubiquitous undershirts—
not T-shirts, those were for another class, another age,
but undershirts—sleeveless, white and ribbed,
and their beer bellies drooping.

They were factory workers, all of them, every one, employees of
American Steel, Republic Steel, Jones and Laughlin,

Hanna Paints, Glidden Paints, Addressograph-Multigraph,
Van Dorn Iron, U.S. Aluminum, Picker X-Ray,
Allied Chemical, Apex Motors, White Motors,
Cleveland Hardware, Clark Controller, Cleveland Welding,
Ferro Manufacturing, Eberhard Manufacturing,
Eton Manufacturing, Chase Brass, Cleveland Graphite,
Vulcan Tool and Die, Tinnerman Speednut,
American Spool and Wire;
house after double house, street after street,
Italians, Lithuanians, Slavs, Poles, Hungarians, Slovaks,
neighborhood pressed against neighborhood,
and union men every one,
United Steel Workers of America,
United Chemical Workers of America,
United Sheet Metal Workers of America,
UAW, UEW,
AFL and CIO,
every one.

When the evening began to darken and they felt the cool air on
    their naked arms,
the people went inside and turned on their televisions.
But when my Uncle Freddy left the porch, he passed through the
    living room into the kitchen where, maybe,
he took down from the cupboard a new pack of Camels,
then moved slowly, almost shuffling, to the hallway,
the bathroom in front of him, the bedroom to his right, and to
    his left, the spare bedroom, his den.

Maybe he paused there in the hallway for a moment, and slowly
    opened the new pack of cigarettes, slowly lit one,
wheezed his emphysemic wheeze a time or two,
and waited to smell the heavy tobacco smoke mix with the
    smells of supper's tomato sauce and pasta.
Then he turned toward the door of his den
and closed himself inside that room for the evening.

I was only in his den a couple of times;
once would have been enough.
Forty years later that place is as vivid to me as the mountains are
   outside my window at this moment.

II

Stand in the doorway. Step in.
Turn right and face the outside wall.
There is one window in the middle with a dark green shade,
the kind for keeping out all light, perhaps left over from the
   blackouts during the war. The shade is always drawn.
Old and dirty, green and silver wallpaper is on the wall, as on all
   the walls in this room.
To the right of the window, a calendar with a photograph of a
   mostly naked woman.
Her lips are pursed. She stares outward, a catatonic stare,
the kind Kim Novak stared at William Holden from the swing in
   the park in the motion picture *Picnic*.

Turn left and face another wall. There is a day-bed up against this
   one; it is also green but darker than the walls.
Next to it, to the left, a little wooden keg, and on top of it is a
   stack of worn copies of *Saga* and *Field & Stream*.
Uncle Freddy never read anything but *Saga* and *Field & Stream*—
he never read the newspaper.

Tacked to the wall above the couch is a fake leopard skin, cut from
   some car upholstery, and hooked to it,
dangling treacherously, are a dozen fishing lures:
musky baits, big ones,
some of them a foot long, looking ludicrous and mean.
They hang there waiting for water, action,
a monstrous fish gored through the mouth,
thrashing and boiling the lake behind the boat,
a man, my Uncle Freddy, at the other end of the line, his teeth
   clenched in battle,

30

his lips slightly smiling, his blood banging against his temples.

And above the leopard skin and baits, also fastened to the wall, are
    two fishing rods and reels, crossed like swords.

Turn left again and face another wall.
High up in the right-hand corner, where the ceiling and the walls
    converge, a minnow seine
drapes gracefully halfway to the center of the ceiling,
filling the corner and sagging almost halfway to the floor.
The soft curves of the brown netting make a hammock, and in the
    hammock
a few pieces of water-worn cork and a piece of gray, feather light
    driftwood rest gently, in a stillness they must have known
once on a summer evening, the sun going down, water lapping
    against the shore.

In the center of this wall stands Uncle Freddy's gun cabinet.
Once, maybe twice, Uncle Freddy had unlocked the glass door
    and let me hold the guns.
There was a .218 Bee with an 8-power Weaver scope for killing
    woodchucks,
and a big 12-gauge Ithaca with a 30-inch barrel and full choke for
    ducks and geese,
and a Winchester 94, a .30-30, for deer.
But the object of my desire, the only one I cared about, was the
    16-gauge, double-barrel, side-by-side, Fox.
The stock and forearm were delicately checkered,
and the dark walnut glistened with a deep patina from years of
    Freddy's oil and rubbing.
At the breech, engraved in the metal, was a tiny hunting scene of
    a man and a dog at point and a partridge exploding away and
    trees and grass, and all that
in a space no more than two inches long by one inch high.
It was a vision of our dream.

I always hoped when Freddy died I'd get that 16-gauge, but I

31

didn't. I didn't even get it after Aunt Gertrude died.

All the guns were immaculately clean. They looked new, and the truth is, they were; none had ever been fired.

Freddy kept the shells and cartridges in a small drawer at the bottom of the gun cabinet.
There was one box of shells for each gun, four boxes, four different kinds of shells. And each box was full,
but the boxes were tattered and worn from years of having the cartridges taken out and handled and put back again.

III

Freddy and I went hunting together only once.
It was a Saturday, and we drove an hour and a half to Joe Paluchek's place in Ashtabula.
Paluchek worked at the plant with Uncle Freddy, but he had moved away from the East Side, had gotten out,
had bought ten acres in the country, or what went for country on the edges of Cleveland.
Paluchek was the envy of his friends. He had a crummy house on a crummy ten acres, but it was land and it was his.
I'd heard about him for years. He was the guy who could piss off his back porch and go hunting in his own back yard.
An hour and a half drive from home to work, one way, was not too much to pay, and everybody knew it.

Joe came out to greet us. He was standing very straight and his chest, it seemed to me, was puffed out.
He took Uncle Freddy by the hand, slapped him on the back and said: Welcome to the country!
And Uncle Freddy looked around and said, all the way into the kitchen: You sure got a nice place here, Joe.
And Joe said: Well, it ain't much, but it's mine and it's home and I can piss off my back porch and hunt in my own back yard.

32

And Freddy smiled and shook his head.

We sat at the kitchen table and had coffee and doughnuts and the
    two men talked and I listened.
They did not talk about the union or the plant.
They talked about hunting and game and their guns and about
    a fishing trip they thought they should take next summer.
Finally Joe thought it was time to get going, so we put on our
    hunting clothes;
the two men loaded their shotguns—I didn't have a gun—and we
    struck off into the field behind the house.

It was a hot November day and dusty.
After what seemed like a very short time, Joe kicked up a
    cottontail and killed it, almost blowing it in half.
Joe said it was a good sign, that the game was on the move today,
but we thrashed through that little field the rest of the morning
    and never saw another living thing.

Joe's property line at the back was a chain-link fence,
    and beyond the fence there was a graveyard of sorts for old
    tractor-trailer rigs,
a couple of acres probably, paved over with cement that was now
    heaved and cracked with age,
where dozens of old tractors and trailers stood, rusting and dented,
    with flat tires or no tires at all and broken windshields
and some broken beer bottles, and all this was silent and still,
except maybe in a slight breeze the back door to one of the trailer
    rigs would creak slightly on its rusting hinges.

I stood for a long time, the others having gone on, with my
    fingers hooked into the fence and stared
at the place beyond, the clutter and rubble. I turned away
and moved through the grimy little field toward the men.

IV

It was almost dark when we got back to Alhambra Street.
Joe had given us the rabbit, and we had laid it out gently on some
  newspaper in the trunk.
By the time Uncle Freddy had parked the car in the driveway and
  opened the trunk, a half dozen neighbors
were standing around waiting to see what we had to show.
Everyone was strangely quiet
as they stared down on the blood-soaked fur of the cottontail.

A rabbit, a wild rabbit, here, on Alhambra Street, in Cleveland,
  Ohio,
an animal that just this morning had lived in a field, slept under a
  bush, drunk from a brook,
an animal that lived far away, in the country, in Ashtabula.
For a moment these workers in factories had been drawn away
into a common past, to a time when they were all hunters, all
close to the country, and their reverential silence was for that time
  long ago
and for the sense of loss they all felt at being who and where they
  were now.

We gutted and skinned the rabbit, took it upstairs to the kitchen,
  quartered it, put it to soak, and went into the den,
where we cleaned the gun, even though it had not been fired,
and put it back in the gun cabinet and locked the door.

V

Turn left again and face the fourth and final wall.
On the right is the door.
Attached to the rest of the wall is a long workbench
with a grindstone and a vise bolted to it and resting on it an
  ashtray, two hunting knives and some fishing tackle.
There is a swivel chair on casters, the kind secretaries use or
  people who do delicate piecework on assembly lines.

Above the workbench is the focus of the entire room.
A painting, a reproduction of an oil, big, four foot by two, on
    cardboard with those squiggly lines to make it look like brush
    strokes,
of the Rockies, maybe the Tetons, with half their height above
    tree line and snow on the top, even now in early fall,
and in the foreground
a mountain meadow with flowers, asters maybe, blue anyway,
and in the middle ground a glacial lake, a reflecting mirror for the
    mountains,
and on the lake, resting like a dragonfly or an aspen leaf,
a canoe with a man in it fishing, alone, alone
in this vast and pristine wilderness.

There are two spotlights attached to the ceiling that shine down
    on the painting
so that Uncle Freddy can sit in the swivel chair in the dark,
and be lost.

I can see him, my Uncle Freddy,
sitting in his swivel chair, in the dark,
spotlights on the picture, his rifle or shotgun in his hands.
I can see him turn in the chair, quickly, snap the gun to his
    shoulder, and:
Pow! He says: Pow!

Again and again, night after night, year after year,
I see him turning in his chair. Or fishing on that lake,
his fly line unfurling, slowly, as in a dream, gracefully
curving, laying out, settling softly, lightly
on the skin of the water.

I see him in the double house on Alhambra Street, in his den,
trapped forever, condemned to work a lathe at Picker X-Ray,
to spend his nights turning in that chair, around and around
in his dream on Alhambra Street,

turning, turning,
my Uncle Freddy,
and I hear him saying:
Pow!

He says:
Pow!

ANTOINE ON HUNTING AND SOME SPOOKS

David, you go hauntin'? I be.
Now I got annuder moud to feed.
Gonna plug a gov'ment beef.
Don't care if it be a skipper needer.
I ain't haunt dem hardwood ra'bits
since I was a boy, since dat time one fall
dose downcountry killers stay to our place.
T'ree of 'em, all out back tagedder in a baunch,
see a big ol' bauck, all fire to once,
fill dat poor ol' basterd up,
but he keep on goin', jomp over da fence,
hang all his gut out on da wire
but keep goin'. Poor ol' basterd.
Whan I see dat, I quit. Dunno why.

I haf' a version of dat deer dat night,
see him in my dream just like a spook.
He keep on raunin', den he turn araoun'
an' raun right thru dem basterds
an' keep on goin'.
I still see 'im all dese years afder
and' he *still* goin'.

Dat make me t'ink about our haunted house.

When I be a pup we caum daown fraum Derby
move to our place.

Da ol' spooks don' like da way we put da furniture.
We lay in bed a' night an' hear 'em daown da stairs
movin' da furniture araound da way dey like it.
We have da priest caum over bless da house;
he say spooks is friendly
all dey wan' is for da furniture
to be da way dey like it.
So we let 'em put it where dey wan'
an' ever't'ing be okay. Julluk 'at.

Only ol' Babe Williams never caum into da house.
He work daown to da cemetery too many years.
He wear 'is hat to bed to keep da spooks out.
He caum over to our place
haf'ta give 'im supper on da porch.
Won't caum in.

Now ol' Babe is dead 'n' gone
just like dat old bauck
an' naow I see 'em bod' tagedder in my dream.

Just last night I seen 'em raunin' side by side
up da road. See right tru em bot'.
You'd t'ink dat be a scary dream
but it wan't.
I like to see 'em raunin' der tagedder.

An' dey was talkin' to each odder
while dey ran.

✦ ✦ ✦

JIMMY

Jimmy is thirty, an only child, still lives at home
with his mother and his father and works the farm with them.
I might never have known him if my car hadn't broken down
one time just outside East Judevine. Jimmy stopped
and fixed it. We got to be sort of friends.
I don't see him all that much but when I do
we visit. We like each other.

At first glance Jimmy looks retarded, but he's not;
it's just that he still moves awkward like a boy.
His head is too big for his body
and his dark eyes and hair—his grandpa's French—
make his round face seem oddly sunken.
He has two fingers missing from one hand,
an accident on the farm.

Jimmy is a good farmer, better than his father,
but probably he'll spend his life working on the home place
and come up to fifty with nothing.
It would be just like his father to die and will the place
to someone else.

When I talk to Jimmy, we always talk about machines.
Jimmy loves machines; he's a good mechanic too,
better than his father.

The one time I saw him dressed up was down at the church
for his uncle's wedding.
He was trying to do the right thing so he walked around
like a tin soldier, a permanent smile pasted on his face.
His fly was down.

When Jimmy talks he holds his hands on edge in the air,
fingers tight together, and moves them in little jerks

from side to side as if
they were fish
trying to swim through grease.
He swallows hard at the end of every phrase.

When you pass him on the road and he waves
he raises his hand flat and forward, fingers still
tight together and his face is stern, almost fearful,
like a Byzantine Jesus offering benediction.

We don't visit all that much but when we do it's hard for me
because
there is something I always want to ask him, something
I want to blurt out, drop the talk of carburetors
and say: Jimmy, what do you do for sex?

He's thirty, lives at home, upstairs, over his parents' room.
There's no woman for him anywhere. He never goes out.
His parents never take him anywhere.
He never sees any of his old high-school friends,
if he ever had any.

I want to say, Jimmy! I want to know. Do you still take
your penis in your hand? How often? Where? In your room
after mother and father have gone to sleep? Do you ride
your snow machine into the woods and do it there?
Don't you want a woman? When you go down to Morrisville
to the feed store where that girl works at the counter,
when you could reach over, touch her—
what do you think about?
Is milking cows dawn and dark enough for you?
Is your snow machine enough?
Do you ever dream of something else?

Or maybe you are happy. Maybe you like it there at home.
What's so very wrong with that?

Or is it, Jimmy, in your thirty years you've come to be
a kind of slave, a eunuch,
in the fields of your lord
and father.

ENVOY TO JIMMY

First I've got to tell you
there's only one radio station around here
anybody ever listens to
because it's the one with the farm news
and the local news and the Trading Post
and comes on at five so folks have music to milk cows by.

Everybody listens to it while they're going down the road.
It's nice because
everybody's head bounces to the same tempo.

I was coming home one day up the river road
and saw Jimmy coming toward me in the pickup
headed for the sawmill or the feed store.

I was going to toot and wave, I always do,
mostly everybody does. Then I saw him
in the cab in that instant
as we passed each other
his arms stretched straight against the wheel,
his head thrown back, eyes almost closed,
his mouth   wide   with song.

ALBERT

Like Edith says:
Albert Putvain's a no good wuthless pup,
ain't too swift neither.
When he was clearin' land 'raound his trailer
he caught the corner of the place wi' the crawler blade
an' tore the bedroom off.
But that ain't nathin', when he was young he and his brother
was workin in the woods
an' Albert backed a crawler right up over top his brother,
squashed 'im flat, killed 'im,
an' it ain't never seemed ta bother Albert any.

Why, he don't know when ta quit.
Him sixty-five and a fifth wife an' a baby girl.
Why, he's got kids from here ta Brattleboro.
Prab'ly the on'y thing he ever learned ta do
so he jes' keeps doin' it.

An' those tew ol' state guys he boards up in that ol' bus,
poor re-tards,
they'd be better off back daown to the hospital,
an Albert sayin':
Ah mik 'im walk da woads so dey won't git wazy.
Why, you know he's makin' money off that thing,
you know he is.
Albert knows more ways a makin' money doin' nathin'
'an the whole rest athe world put together.
But they c'ught 'im too, didn't they?
Last year, one week, got convicted thirteen times
of welfare frawd.

Albert is also an architect.
He has garnished his trailer, as many people do,
with porches and sheds and lean-tos and a garage

41

so that now you can't even see the trailer
it's so buried in the rubble of his invention.

He has an old hay knife painted silver suspended from wires
hanging over the garage door and a silver sickle and a
silver milk can with a gilded colonial eagle perched
on top of it. In the dooryard there is a whorl
of flower pots with plastic red and white carnations
hanging from the tines of an old hay rake.

Watching over all of this are six pink flamingos
on wire legs, each standing and nodding in the wind.
And out front, perpendicular to the road,
so you can see it good,
there's a hand painted sign that glows in the dark
and says:

Mr. Putvain.

THE TWO OLD GUYS AT ALBERT'S

There are two retarded guys from the state hospital
boarded in a bus at Albert's. I don't know their names.
Nobody does. Albert never takes them anywhere.
Maybe the state told him not to; I don't know.
It's not much. An old bus to sleep in, nothing to do
but walk the road and shovel snow, bounce a ball
for Albert's kid in the afternoon, listen to each other
masturbate at night. Not much, but better than the hospital.

The ward   a room   crowded with fifty beds
twenty-five on either wall.   The old men who lie   all day
on their sides   all facing   the same way
so no one has to face   another.   Their only cooperation.

The old men who lie   all day   and say nothing
look at   nothing.   The kid   fourteen   who rocks all day
in a chair   that doesn't rock.   Cold coffee
from a peanut butter jar.   The smell of men
who wet their pants.   Stale tobacco air.   Dark halls.
And doors   locked doors.   The moans at night.
And once a day   the doctor
with a hypodermic.

The manic girl across the courtyard   who every day
takes down her pants   and dances   jangling
like a crow   across the porch   crying   like a crow:
Hey Baby!   Hey Baby!   Come over here!
She lifts her dress   and puts   fingers
between her legs   and rubs   twitching   like a crow
until she falls   her wings spread out   her body
shivering   on the porch floor.

You   watching through the window   your penis
in your hands   in a room with fifty others
rubbing   rubbing   while you watch   and while
the attendant   watches you.
Then your hand is sticky   smelling of ammonia.
You wipe it on your pants   front and back
strop it   like a razor.

I have seen men jailed in rooms   all of them   so lost
so alone   that there is nothing—
not a summer rain   not a smile   not a doughnut—
to be shared.   Men like particles of dust suspended
in the air   floating   at random   making
accidentally   without purpose   action and reaction
to no end   men   (like me)   moving   isolated
dumb   unknowing   suspended in the air.

There are these two retarded guys boarded up at Albert's.

You can see them every day walking the road between
their bus and where the hill starts up to Granny's.

The younger one, who looks about fifteen but probably is forty,
tilts and limps as he walks. His mouth
is permanently distorted and his misshapen head shows
that if he ever had a mother
she didn't care enough to roll him in his crib
so his head wouldn't flatten in the back.
When I wave to him he jerks his arm up, stops,
turns his ugly face and smiles.
Then quick, as if someone hollered at him,
he goes on walking,
tilting and limping and walking.

I wonder if he dreams about the manic girl,
if he still sees her in the night,
jangling in her bones, dancing, crying for him
like a crow.

The older one who looks, and probably is, fifty-five
walks straight but keeps his arms out from his sides
stiff and at an angle.
His hands flutter constantly.
When I wave to him his roadside arm rises and falls,
rises and falls,
with the hand fluttering at its end,
but his eyes stay down on the road.
I have never seen his face.
The old guy keeps that up, the arm rising and falling,
the hand trembling at its end.
I can see it in the rearview mirror until I make the bend.

There are two retarded guys boarded up at Albert's.
Every day they walk the road.
They never walk together.

They are always
about a hundred feet apart.

GRANNY

Granny lived down the road from Albert.
She was eighty when she died. Everybody said she was crazy.
Probably she was. She was suspicious of everyone.
She had visions, saw conspiracies, thought every stranger
who came along was out to get her.
She always liked me because I waved when I went by.

Granny had a cleft palate and no teeth.
She was also hard-of-hearing
so when she talked to you she shouted.
Her husband died about ten years ago.
The winter he died the house burnt down.
Granny spent the last decade of her life alone
living in a springhouse and a camper trailer.
She milked ten cows every day, twice a day,
to the day she died.
She was obsessed with the memory of her husband, Lee.
She talked about him constantly
and when she did
she moaned a nasal, toothless, hair-lipped moan.

Granny had a dream of selling out, moving
to Morrisville to manage an apartment building.
She lived her dream and sold her place about twice a year.
She'd have a lawyer draw a deed and bill of sale,
then at exactly the last moment, she'd back out.
Nobody ever had the heart, thank God,
to make her follow through.
Everybody understood how Granny was.

Once a guy from Hardwick
who didn't know what buying land from Granny really meant
actually got a cattle truck of Holsteins to the barn.
The neighbors could see what was coming
so we stopped by to watch the show.
The guy climbed down out of the cab all smiles.
Granny was waiting for him, the bill of sale in her hand.
She hollered something at him about her husband,
then lit the bill of sale and threw it at him.
After that she didn't sell the place so much.

Granny couldn't leave. The day the house burnt down
Lee's ghost left the house and went to living in the barn.
She couldn't leave Lee's ghost.

Granny never did anybody any harm.

A few years ago, in August, after haying,
a woman we had met at a party in Craftsbury came to see us.
She had a kid with her, a guy about eighteen.
They were driving an old Pontiac station wagon.
There were four dogs in the back.
They parked at the foot of the drive.
The car's shocks were gone and even after they got out,
the car still bobbed and shivered in its place
like a tin behemoth with Parkinson's disease.

They staggered up the hill to the house.
They were high or drunk or both.
It was ten o'clock in the morning.
We drank some of their wine; then they drove off
down the road toward the village.

Later I found out they stopped at Granny's place.
Granny was in the pasture
graining a heifer she had staked under a maple tree.

They jumped out of the car
and ran across the pasture to the old woman.
She was a total stranger to them.
They hugged her and kissed her and shouted wildly:
Power to the people! Power to the people!
They told Granny they were going to give her lots of money
and that she'd never have to work again.
Granny broke away from them and ran into the barn
and hid in the hayloft. Bobbie found her up there
that evening after dark.

The woman from Craftsbury and her friend came back
once more that summer.
This time Granny was in the barn when they pulled up.
She ran out the back, across the pasture, through a swamp
and hid in the high grass of Rufus Chaffee's orchard
all afternoon.

Granny died last spring, in the morning
while she was doing chores.
Bobbie found her about noon, lying in the gutter,
the milking machine still pulsating in her hand
and the cows blatting from the pain of stretched udders.

I miss Granny. I miss her angry voice.
I miss her plaintive wail for Lee.

I remember the first time I ever met Granny.
I was bucking firewood one fall, some maples
the power company had let down
along the lane into Uncle Clyde's.
Granny shuffled over from her trailer on the hill.
She was furious.

'ut 'er 'ooin! 'ew 'ow 'ut 'er 'ooin?
'ems 'ah 'ees! 'oo 'ol 'ew 'ew 'ou'd 'ut 'em?

'ut 'er 'ooin! 'ems 'ah 'ees!
'iss 'ah 'an', ain't 'yde's!
I 'ew 'ief 'ee?
Ah'm an ol' 'oman, 'even'y-'ix 'ears ol'
'ah 'us'un's 'ead. 'ah 'oaus 'urnt ou'.
'ah 'if a'on i' a 'ing'oaus an' a 'ailer,
'ah 'ik 'en 'aows.
'ah əh 'et i!

I apologized. Told her I didn't mean to steal her trees.
Said I thought they were Clyde's. Granny mellowed
and ended telling me I was welcome to the wood.

'er 'el'um 'ew 'at 'ood.
ah'm 'ad 'er 'ew 'ew 'ave ih.
Ih 'ew 'eed ih, ah'm 'ad 'er 'ew 'ew 'ave ih.
'er 'ik'd on 'iss 'ill. Ah 'een 'ew 'o i.
'ew 'ave.
'er 'ik'd on 'iss 'ill.
Ah'm 'ad 'er 'ew 'ew 'ave ih.

Then she began about her husband, Lee.
It was the first time I'd ever heard her lament.
Her vowels elongated. She lengthened all her final sounds,
syncopated all her phrases. She moaned. She wailed.
She rolled her head and sang.

Oh, ah 'ish   'ew'd 'et   ah 'us'un', 'ee!
'ee uz ah 'icest 'an   'at e'er 'od   in 'ews!
'ee um 'alkin' 'oun ah 'oad   un 'ay,   'opped in
'an 'e'er 'eft.
'ow 'e's 'ead!
Ah 'us'un's 'ead!
An' ah'm an ol' 'woman,   'even'y-'ix 'ears ol',
ah 'us'un's 'ead!
Ah 'oaus 'urnt ou',

ah 'if a' on i' a 'ing'oaus an a 'ailer,
ah 'ik 'en 'aows,
ah əh 'et i!

Ah 'us'un's 'ead!
'ee's 'ead!

an ah'm   a'oun!

A TRANSCRIPTION OF GRANNY'S MONOLOGUES

What you doing! You know what you're doing?
Them's my trees! Who told you you could cut them?
What you doing! Them's my trees!
This my land, ain't Clyde's!
Why you grief me?
I'm an old woman, seventy-six years old.
My husband's dead. My house burnt out.
I live alone in a springhouse and a trailer.
I milk ten cows.
I just get by!

◆

You're welcome to that wood.
I'm glad for you to have it.
If you need it, I'm glad for you to have it.
You're liked on this hill. I seen you go by.
You wave.
You're liked on this hill.
I'm glad for you to have it.

◆

Oh, I wish   you'd met   my husband, Lee.

49

.e nicest man   that ever trod   in shoes.
   e walking down the road   one day   stopped in
  er left.
  ιe's dead!
My usband's dead!
And I'm an old woman,   seventy-six years old
my husband's dead.
My house burnt out,
I live alone in a springhouse and a trailer.
I milk ten cows,
I just get by!

My husband's dead!
Lee's dead!

And I'm   alone!

✦ ✦ ✦

FORREST

Forrest died five years ago.
I never really knew him.
But I saw him, almost daily, winter and summer,
flapping down the Dunn Hill road toward the family graves
up where Hermie used to live.

I could see him loping,
taking those huge strides as if he were
angrily running after
a child,
his old gray overcoat dragging
on the gravel,

and that World War One
aviator's hat
flapping at his ears.

GOING PLACES

Eighty-six years ago Forrest squeezed between his mother's thighs
and stayed   on the farm   where he arrived,   and he died
where he was born:
A life of work and watching in that place,
the same house, same view out the windows,
same sidehill pasture, garden, fields and barn,
woodlot, brook and meadow.

According to our way of thinking, the Zapotecs were crazy not to make use of the wheel when they knew of its existence. The curious thing is that they had wheels, but only for toys. . . . They were in a word perfectly capable of "inventing the wheel" but for some reason (which must remain

to us profoundly mysterious) they never bothered with it. They were not
interested in going places.

Thomas Merton
Ishi Means Man

He grew there, became a man, took over, married,
raised a family, traveled widely over his two hundred acres,
but never left the state.

Except that once,
a downcountry friend took him to the ocean in Connecticut.
He walked across the beach to the edge of continent and sea,
dipped his fingers in the surf, tasted of it, turned and said:
It's salty. Let's go home.

Except for that he hardly left the county.

Zapotec or neighbor, three thousand years ago in Mexico
or yesterday just down the road, the image clings,
proof of our dissatisfaction, our longing
for a time when going places didn't mean a thing,
when we could do our work and know
some comfort in our skins.

SARAH

It wasn't Sarah's idea to come up here. Timothy's the one
who wanted to quit a good job in the bank,
give up his suits and ties and dress shoes
and go north into the wilderness so he could fulfill some kind of
boy's dream of working in the woods.

Sarah had been happy where she was, in Connecticut, or happy
    enough, if happiness has anything to do with it,
but she'd come nevertheless out of obligation or indifference,

she didn't know, nor did she care.

All she knew was, she was here now, dumped out here in the
    middle of nowhere.
All day alone in that old farmhouse while Timothy
staggered around in the snowy woods in his boots and heavy shirts
and coveralls reeking of gas and oil, sweat and pitch.
Not exactly what Sarah had had in mind for the rest of her life.

In the hours of her isolation and her loneliness, day after day,
Sarah became aware that she was more than merely bored.
Her life was meaningless, without a purpose, which struck her
    oddly
that she would worry over such things as purpose and meaning
since such concerns were not a part of the material and
    consumptive, self-indulgent lap of opulence
out of which she had come.

Then Sarah realized that these new and odd concerns had come to
her because of her friendship with Ann and Raymond.

Raymond and Ann farmed a small farm on the other side of the
    hill, and on the far side of huge and desolate Bear Swamp.
Raymond and Ann were kind and warm, open and generous,
and when Timothy and Sarah first arrived
they took the two young people into their lives
and made them feel wanted and at home.

At first it was Timothy who leapt into the friendship learning
    from them
all he could about gardening, wood heat, the myriad details of
    how to live
in the country and in the north. But as time passed and Timothy
had gotten from them what he wanted, he lost interest in them,
while Sarah, for reasons at first she couldn't understand, initiated

an ever-deepening contact
with the older couple.

As Sarah grew more and more attached to Raymond and Ann,
    she began to think of them as trees
rooted and growing in that place, these two
whose lives seemed so considered and complete, as if their lives
were a dream of what human life could be.

In the afternoons when she is alone in her house,
Sarah goes into the bedroom,
opens the curtains across the window that looks out on the
meadow and the mountains,
lies down on the bed and stares across the snowy fields,
the blank and empty whiteness,
into the purpling winter afternoon,
and she weeps,
for the loneliness she feels, for the emptiness she knows,
which is so much greater than the emptiness beyond the window.

Timothy tired of his childhood dream and went back to
    Connecticut,
back to the bank, but Sarah stayed on alone in Judevine.

After a time a young man moved in with Sarah, stayed awhile,
and then was gone. Then there was another and another.

Then a woman came to stay whose name was Breeze Anstey.
Breeze and Sarah started an herb farm and sustained
their business and their life together for a few years,
but that liaison ended also, and Sarah, as she had done before,
stayed on alone.

RAYMOND AND ANN

I

Raymond and Ann kept to themselves and because of that
some people thought them snooty and aloof. It wasn't true.
Other people theorized perhaps there'd been
some great pain in their lives, more than
the stillborn child buried on the knoll
above their house, that kept them from the usual
sociability. No one knew. Personally, I think when they came
to this mountain fifty years ago they wanted
only silence and each other and having found
these things they were happy.

Raymond was God's gardener. He grew the best of everything,
his garden always free of weeds, rows so straight
it seemed he planted with a transit.

Although they were poor and everything about the place
homemade, their farm had neatness and an order
reflective of people who know what to do and how to do it
and who do not overstretch the limits of their land
or themselves.

By the time I knew them they were old and didn't have a team,
only Sandy, middling size, mostly Belgian, who weighed
maybe seventeen hundred pounds and was so intelligent
if she'd had hands she would have harnessed herself,
intuited the day's work and done her jobs unattended.
I always had the feeling that, though there were other animals—
cows, chickens, sheep, a pig—there was an absolute equality
between the man, the woman, and the horse.

Raymond was tall, angular and bony.
He carried himself upright to his dying day.

He cackled when he laughed and when he told a joke
he always laughed *before* the punch line
so he could be the first.

Ann was slim and quick, full breasts and hips,
and although her face was plain, she was to me
unspeakably beautiful. She wore her white hair
and wrinkled skin the way a summer flower wears its bloom.
And in her eyes, even at the age of seventy, burnt a fire
so bright and fierce, a passion so intense,
it made me feel old and worn. In her presence
I was sick at the slackness of my life.

II

Every afternoon after dinner Raymond and Ann
lay down together on the large sofa in the living room,
wrapped themselves around each other and took a nap.

Sometimes they slept, sometimes they only lay
in the stillness listening. In summer they listened
to the wind and the birds' songs. In winter
they listened to the wind and the mute birds—little feet
scuttling across the feeder on the windowsill. Often
they fell into a half-sleep in which they dreamed
waking dreams or they let their minds go still as the room.

They napped like this each day because it was a time
when they could come together, these two distinctly separate
people, touch each other and be very nearly one being
in that place.

They had an unspoken understanding that during these times
they wouldn't talk, but one day Ann said: You know,
we've been more than fifty years, doing the same things
day after day, changing only with the seasons and I've never

got tired of it, oh, angry and frustrated, plenty,
but never tired. I wonder if we ever will.

Raymond chuckled: Well, we had better get to it
if we're going to; we don't have much time left.

They both saw clearly and briefly then
the end of their lives and they laughed quietly
and held each other.

III

I was thinking just now, Raymond said, about that time,
years ago, after we built this place. I could see the two
of us lying on the sofa and I remembered clearly how we looked
and what I thought. We were young and new and I held you here
as we are now and I was thinking, I wonder what it will be like
to be here when we're old, the two of us in shrinking bodies
wrapped around each other. I think I knew then, fifty years ago,
pretty clearly what it would be like today. I knew
how it would feel. Do you think that means our lives
have been too predictable?

Why should it?

Well, to see that far ahead and then get to where you saw
and look back and see you were right
seems so strange, predictable.

Have you enjoyed it?

You know I have.

I have too.

IV

Toward the end of the sixties and into the early seventies
every summer there was what Antoine called a "hippie invasion"
around here. Young people from the cities poured into
these hills. I remember one spring Antoine saying:

Watch out! boys. Dere really caumin' in dis summer.
Dere's gonna be a million of 'em wash in here like a tidal
wa'f. Dis place use' to be more caows 'an people,
now we're gonna be more hippies 'an caows!

Raymond and Ann became mentors to them,
elders with Confucian knowledge, replacements
for the parents the kids had left behind.
Raymond and Ann were visions of another way of life.

But the influence went both ways and Raymond took
to working in the garden barefooted,
then he went shirtless and got a summer tan,
then he removed his cap and the traditional
bronzed forehead with abrupt demarcation
between the sunburn and the ashen skull disappeared.
It was the talk of the town. What was he doing
at sixty-something acting like a kid?
It tickled Ann, and what other people said
didn't bother her at all. It never had.

One summer afternoon Raymond came in from the garden,
approached Ann from behind, put his arms around her middle
and kissed the back of her neck. Then his forearms touched
her breasts dangling unsupported beneath her shirt.
And her shirt was open from the top a few buttons.

Goodness, what is this?

What is what?

This.

His hands moved to her breasts and held them.

Well, maybe you shouldn't be thinking you're the only one
can learn from hippies. If you go around with half your clothes
still on the hook, I guess I can leave half mine in the drawer.

Well, I guess you can!

Raymond rested his chin on her shoulder
and gazed down her shirt.

Does it feel good?

Sort of strange would be more like it.

Do you like it?

Some.

Would you go out in public the way you are right now?

Raymond Miller, you know I'm not a hussy!

V

They were under the dooryard apple tree at the summer table
shelling peas when they heard the noise.
Early July, the height of summer, clear and warm
and a light breeze to stir things, cool things,
an idle day filled with ease, gentle and sweet
and a rarity in this ungentle place.
A half-dozen days a year like this, no more, the others

59

always with some kind of edge to them, a harshness,
which makes it all the more wonder-filled that this place
could yield two people such as Ann and Raymond.

At first a dull roar in the distance, then closer and louder
until when it passed through the sugarbush just down the road,
it had to it the sound of war. Then they were there:
four of them. Four steel helmets gleaming black,
four faces with dark glasses, four faces pale, ashen, as if
they had been powdered. In black they came:
black leather jackets, leather pants, leather boots,
leather gloves with gauntlets to the elbows and silver rivets
gleaming everywhere, their bikes black and silver too—
choppers, handlebars in the air, seats leaning back—
they roared into the lane and toward the house and garden.

The chickens scratching in the dooryard screamed
and ran away; Sandy reared and bolted, broke through the fence
and disappeared into the woods.

In black they came, into the garden, into the rows of corn,
over tomatoes, down rows of broccoli, through the fence of peas.
They wheeled and turned and came again, through the garden
    flowers,
over squash and cucumbers, dill and thyme, carrots, potatoes,
beans. One rider singled out an errant hen and ran her down.
They came again through the garden, their tires
churning and digging the earth, spewing soil and broken plants
into the air. They roared toward the two old people
then veered away, down the lane, down the road,
over the hill and away.

VI

After supper on a summer evening.
They were sitting in the cool house, she in his easy chair.

She looked up at him quizzically; already she had left him,
was in a strange place, alone. He watched the life
drain from her face. She said nothing—
not even good-bye.

He sat for a time in the growing dusk and stillness.
Then, as the sun headed down behind the mountains,
he scooped her into his arms the way you would a child
fallen asleep somewhere away from its bed and laid her down
on the sofa where she liked to nap.

He went to the barn and finished chores,
then stepped into the evening and felt the cold air
spilling down the sidehill all around him. He listened
to the crickets, the barred owl and white-throated sparrow,
the wood thrush. Then he came inside and went to bed.

In the first light of morning he dug a grave on the knoll
behind the house next to the child's grave, then went to the barn
and built a box of rough pine boards from his store of lumber.
He harnessed Sandy and she drug the box to the knoll
and with her help he lowered it into the grave.

He went into the house and picked her up. He wrapped his arms
around her middle and carried her upright, her head rising above
his head because she was stiff.
He put her in the box, put on the lid and nailed it down.
He covered her over. He filled the grave.

He sat down on the freshly mounded earth
and began rocking slowly back and forth.
And then he wept.
His tears poured down. He moaned and wailed.
He rolled his head and wept.
He shook his fist at heaven. He rose and paced and wept.
He held his face in his hands. He clawed his pants,
tore at his shirt. He stomped the earth and smashed a fist

into an open palm. He turned his face toward heaven
clinched his teeth
and screamed.

When there were no tears left, when he was weak and trembling,
he led Sandy to the barn, unharnessed her,
turned her out to pasture
and went into the house.

He stood at the window then, looking at the mountains,
and he wept again,
this never-ending, accumulated grief
for the inevitable.

POEM FOR A MAN WHOSE WIFE HAS DIED

You can see him in his house
sitting in a chair
his hands folded in his lap
his mouth slightly open.

You can see him in his house
standing at a window
one hand of fingers touched gently
to his lower lip.

You can see him in his house
moving from room to room
his hand trailing his wife's ghost
like a child's blanket.

✦ ✦ ✦

CRAZY TWO-FOOT MAKES IT ROUND AGAIN

The year turns toward itself until it joins itself
and makes beginning end. It makes a circle not a line,
and held within that closure, in the crush of breaths and flesh
is a man, turning in the turning year, bending as all breaths bend
toward the dead, his flesh toward soil.

NOVEMBER

Where do you enter a circle?
When there is no beginning where do you break in?
Say November. Here. Enter through the emptiness.

Sere gray. Sere brown. The bare trees,
their skinny fingers darkened by the rain, stretch
against the sky. The earth is dank and chill
as an old deserted cellar. Barren. Without song.
The sky is empty, the birds are gone.
Everything is waiting in the rain.

Five o'clock: almost dark. Chimney smoke lies down,
crawls across the meadow like a slow, soft snake.
And he, just come in from the woods, stands watching.
The cold fog is silver on his woolen shirt.

Bank on bank of clouds, like the folds of a shroud,
layer over the mountains.
The sky steals light from both ends of the day.
This is the day the lead gray sky comes down.
Say good-bye to the ground. In the morning: white.
It will snow all night tonight.

DECEMBER

Where there was darkness there is light.
See how morning floods his house.
See the sunlight bounding off the snowy earth,
leaping through the windows. How could such dark create
this bright and lucid day? This must be another place.
It couldn't be the same.

Cold and crystal air. There!
Ravens catch the wind and soar
like hawks.
Blonk. Blonkblonk.
Blonk. Blonk.

Further on toward evening, in the dying light, a human figure
ambles down the road, his hands jammed deep into his pockets,
his white breath streaming behind him like a scarf.

Snow. Featherfluff. Enough to crush the world.
Of itself on itself, layer on layer white.

One fence post tilts above the snow.
The tip of a ship gone down
in this white sea.

JANUARY

Mid night: moon bright:
minus twenty-two degrees
and the man
walks the swamp road to feel
the hair in his nostrils freeze.

Crack and crunch.
A dog lopes across the crusted moonlit snow.
From his jaw a deer leg bobs and dangles.

In the silver dark chimney smoke rises
a hundred feet toward the Pleiades
then flattens to a T.

In the middle of the bright and moony night
bobcat comes to drink the spring's clear water.

No cloud for weeks. He can see the stars at noon.
The moon-cold sun burns for nothing.
A white desert: arid: still.

Red polls scratch and twitter.
Snow buntings rise and swirl and blow away.

Far now the other side of solstice:
forty below and growing colder.
The sound of popping trees.

FEBRUARY

Five o'clock and not yet dark. He sits in the silent house,
drinking tea and watching stove light flow like quiet water.
Everything is old. In the cellar, squash mold, potatoes sprout,
onions fall in upon themselves. And this human flesh too:
brittle as the frozen trees. Beginning at the bottom of his heel
the skin falls powdery on the floor as if flesh really were dust.

If a white cat has one blue eye it'll be
deaf.
If in the middle of the winter the spiders down cellar hang down
it'll be
an early spring.

65

He saw a snowy owl this evening, the two of them come upon
    each other at the end of a day of hunting.
She was sitting on a branch of a tree watching him.
He stopped. They stared at each other; then she
rolled backward off the branch and disappeared
into the darkening trees.

Six o'clock and almost dark. Some animals turn homeward,
others just waking slip into the evening.
Somewhere beyond the meadow
a deer stands up in her snowy bed suddenly afraid.

Too dark. Too cold. Too long. Blue jay, glutton, garish crab,
blue knife of madness, shrieks at the morning.
His cries stab and shatter across the ice.

MARCH

Rain-glaze on snow. Mud and ice and snow.
Coyotes feed themselves on gaunt dreams of spring. Then
what comes slowly suddenly he sees.

Light hovers longer in the southern sky.
Brooks uncover themselves. Alders redden.
Grosbeaks' beaks turn green. Chickadee finds the song
he lost last November, and blue jay abandons
argument and gluttony. He cranes his neck,
bobs his mitered head; he bounces on a naked branch
crying: Spring!
But, like all winter's keepers,
he speaks his dream before
he sees the fact.
Did you hear a phoebe?

And he out again and walking on the earth,
in the air, in the sun, ankle deep in mud.

APRIL

Still no green but slowly now
earth softens to the touch.
Buds stand up like nipples.
The sun beats down.
The death robes shrink
like cellophane before the fire.
Mountain brooks make rage of melting snow.

In the dooryard, the ghosts of winter's grimy rubble rise
like demented souls on Judgment Day:
Glass and rusting cans, broken tires, potato peels, a carburetor,
coffee grounds, tea bags, crankcase oil, a tail pipe, bacon grease,
a hubcap bowl of oily water, wood chips,
a thousand dog turds on the lawn,
plastic bags, onion skins,
the lower jaw of last year's slaughtered pig,
a broken plate, sodden cardboard boxes, gravel on muddy grass,
two deflated pumpkins. The yard is a notebook
where winter's journal wrote itself in litter.

Yet also still this dank and gray. Oh, how he loves
this cold and constant rain, this gray spring,
the chill that keeps him indoors
and the fire going in the stove all day.

He loves this last nod toward the passing dark.
he loves all that is empty, slothful and withdrawn,
this time in which he has a few more days
to stay within himself, and be quiet in his melancholy.

He loves these last days of the barren time
before he has to go outside
and greet the redolent and noisy spring.

Wind and rain.
A rush of wings.
The trees loud again with birds.

Birch and popple catkins droop:
spent penises drip yellow semen
on the air.

Popple and red maple push new leaves.

The geese return.
Their long vees plow the fields of cloud.
High and far away, they are
strange, mysterious as new leaves.

Below them, chickadee, like a friendly hand, remains:
close, diminutive, minimal, half-forgotten
in the bare apple tree.

MAY

In the morning white-throated sparrow cries: The sun! The sun!
I bring the sun in the bright spot beside my eye.
Come out! Come out of your house! The sun has come!

Oh, spring and sun! Song and wing.
The earth redolent of everything!
Including death.

The worst endured, last year's fawn seeks a southern slope,
lays her starven body down and dies in the warming sun.

68

Wind and rain. Wind and rain to shag, loosen, stiffened hearts.
Wind and rain. Wind and rain to rot the corpse.

Gorged, glutted, water-mad the mountain brook
meets the winter-weakened doe takes her, tears her, reddens itself
then scatters the scraps of hide and bone. Tossed up away
the limpid foetus-bones lie caged inside mother's cradle ribs.
Next year's adder's-tongue will sprout
from the empty socket of its eye.
Above a mist, a spirit, like primordial steam streams upward
through the warming rain.

In the woods too. Wolf tree. Den tree. Where the roots go in.
Raccoon, her chin resting softly on crossed paws, her eyes
looking straight ahead: dead.

The earth is pimpled with the dead. These rotting corpses are
her body's phosphorescent jewels. No matter. No matter.
Fertilizer now. All done. Make more with earth and rain and sun.

Earth says to sun: Come seed, come! And he,
hands filled with seed,
moves over the freshly turned earth planting peas and spinach.

Skunk cabbage spears the muck: a furled tip, an artist's brush.
Who's under there? What arm will follow handle?
What mad painter rise to smear the world with green?

Now the round-leafed violet comes, the first point of light,
a yellow mite above the grimy leaves.
And dogtooth violet—trout lily, green-gray, green-brown,
the adder's-tongue—flickers above the ground.
Purple trillium—wake-robin, bloody stinkin' Benjamin—
velvet drapes rich as deer blood coyote spilled on snow.

There. What's left of deer.

No hide. No bone. Just hair
lying soft as milkweed bloom.

Here. The myrtle warbler dressed for spring.
Bright white, blue bright, gray and yellow light,
who doesn't warble at all but cheeps and says:
this is sour, acid soil, is spruce and fir,
is north, is where I make my nest.

There: below him in the wet, brushy place
year after year, generation after generation,
the woodcock whistle and snout.

And there: on only slightly higher ground
the veeries, dreaming they are falling water,
warble and sing their liquid descending glissando,
year after year.

And year after year
always again in the same place
the partridge drums.

And here almost beside him the shy junco
scurries, flits across the ground singing
again this spring only: *tick, tick, tick, tick.*

Lilacs in the dooryard bloom.
The air is sweet as honied tea.
The orchard hums.

JUNE

Seeds break ground. Stretch up. Stretch down.

Now each morning before the sun

two ravens, rulers of the dawn, the sun's black acolytes,
come croaking crying: Day!

Today they saw him watching: a sudden silence:
they wheeled: the hiss and rush of wings.
Gone, withered into the rising sun. And he,
left standing, growing that day's dying shadow.

It is light half the night. It's always day. The sun won't go away.
And green. Darkening green.
The flowers of the world dancing on jade slate.

Cloistered under earth's fertile skin,
the cabbage seed hides a dream of growing inside out,
swelling outward from an inner fire, from
a core tightening daily around its secret heart.

A black fisher cat walked across a black log this morning
his black coat silver in the sunny fog.

JULY

Now each morning, each warm morning,
sunlight on the dew-wet grass, sunlight
on the garden, everything under the sun in these
brief, salubrious days of life and juice and green.

In the steaming swamp in the middle of the day
the snowshoe hare
all brown and summery
cocks his head, listens, scratches lice behind his ear.

In the evening the man stands in his garden and watches the
    vegetables and thinks:
if this group of animals to which he belongs had decided,

in an act of selflessness, of generosity and distance from their idea
of themselves, that the supreme act of creativity and intelligence
    was not to make language or history but instead
to make food by photosynthesis,
why, then, this blue-green broccoli here every day more greatly
    stretching toward the sun would be
the ultimate, the pinnacle, the very top
of the pyramid of being!

He sweats: hayseed stuck in eye-crotch, arm-crotch, crotch.
He stinks, a sweet, thick stink. He loves himself the way he stinks.

Later, because such things happen, suddenly, where field meets
    swamp, without his knowing,
the tractor's cutter bar slipped
under the frightened, frozen bittern and bit her legs—off.
The legless bittern flies away pouring blood across the withering
    grass. She flies away to no perch, to no leg
to stand on.

Two green-and-ruby hummingbirds.
His red shirt.
A flare of yellow lilies.

Blue-eyed grass: green spear and violet eye, a point of yellow iris.

Green pasture.
Orange hawkweed.
Yellow buttercups.

Up before the sun, wading through the bramble
dropping dew-wet, bright red berries into a metal cup.

Oh, praise this life! Praise this world!
Praise and joy for being here—
here with all these others! Alive and here! Praise for all of us!

For everyone!

Hot summer afternoon and he
in the cool and darkened shade of his woodshed
sitting cross-legged on the floor a sharpening stone in his hand
putting an edge on a hoe and from time to time drinking
from his cup of tea and thinking how since time began
men have paused
in the heat of a summer afternoon to rest in the shade
to sharpen a tool, to drink tea.

Then the F-111 flew low over the house and in his dream
he saw a Vietnamese farmer sitting cross-legged in a hut also
on a hot summer afternoon also resting in the shade and also
sharpening a tool and from time to time
drinking from his cup of tea.
And then, in his dream, he saw the other man's house, his family,
his fields, his self all consumed in flames, all—gone
as if they had been washed away in a wave of fire.

And when the man woke from his dream he saw that not himself
nor his family nor his house nor his fields nor any thing
that is there in that place
had been consumed, only his heart consumed in the fire
of his rage.

The next day in the garden he looked at the cabbages and saw
    human skulls.
The beans were disembodied fingers,
the lettuces flaps of human skin,
an ear of corn an unexploded bomb, the squash were land mines
of different shapes and sizes, the tomatoes lumps of bloody flesh
exploding in his hands.

AUGUST

Here: this balsam fir: every internodal, every terminal bud
thousands of them charged with energy and will
seizing the momentary summer
grown thirty inches in sixty days
reaching wildly out
before light fails falls back
drags
cold and dark
over them again.

Slowly the frantic chores of summer wane, the air cools,
and already that autumnal cry of insects floats across the earth—
these fleshy instants of a summer's day plant seed in harvest time
trust their futures to the earth and prepare to go away.

The end of summer and the sun that baked his head
passes coolly now across his shoulders.

Evening:
when day's birds are gone and night's wanderers wait listening
when dark falls softly as a bird's wing, then, beyond the meadow
in the bull spruce a barred owl: *alone   alone   alone*
begins his dark melody to the moon.

In the morning before the dawn
seven heifers
up to their necks in fog
sway and wade supple as cats.

A day of summer rain. Then
in the evening dark it stops and
the moon begins orange and huge
through the branches of the apple tree.

The year, this quick and momentary summer,
tumbles down its long fall toward dark.
Aster and gentian now. The last blue under the sun.

SEPTEMBER

The dawn brings air thin and clear as cellophane.
Under a cloudless sky, the frost passes
through a kingdom that knew only sun and rain,
a gentle people of leaves who ripened fruit all summer.

Tomato corpses droop from assassination stakes, their tender
    bodies riddled by the frost.
The garden is a grave. What vegetables remain
lie fugitive from cold, sequestered underground. Then rain.
Red leaves turn white bellies to the wind.

The year teeters perfectly on light's fulcrum: the equinox.
Then it sinks. In a fog it drowns as in a sea. The varying gray,
the mist, shows each ridge, each spine of mountains separate
from the others, as if row on row of granite breakers caught
in a photograph, in perpetual stillness, might roll again,
might make
a primal, fogbound ocean here—miles from any water.

Now the sun again and the world filling up with color with that
sweet Chinese melancholy in this time of the chrysanthemum.

OCTOBER

A dying time is time to kill. Cow. Chicken. Sheep.
His hands are stained with blood. Carcass on the kitchen table
and he sings softly to himself and scrapes
seven different kinds of flesh
from a pig's skull.

75

The smell of dying leaves, the slanting light
drive him out to kill again.
This time just for fun. Partridge, drumming bird, watch out!

A warm October afternoon the kind they have in paradise.
The bird, the gun explode. Feather ball falls like a wad of dough.
His small beak, his eyes bleed. He beats his breast and makes
snow angels in the leaves. Strange penance, or is it adulation,
for his life as if to drive out quick what little life is left.

He can kill a rabbit too. Hear the rabbit scream. Hear him squeal.
Every fox for miles will be here soon to find only a tiny pool
of blood, some fur and guts.

The killer lopes home through the sweet October yellow light.
He puckers, whistles, his face bright with sun.
He who is alive in the world with these creatures who are dead,
whose round bodies are soft and limp and warm
in the pocket of his coat.

Hush little babies
don't you cry
leaves die too.

This autumnal sadness.

Starshine.
Cold October night.
Cows.
Knee deep in mist.

Now almost all the leaves are down.
Now the popples turning yellow.
Now and last the tamaracks. Everything becoming gray—again.
Again the bare trees their skinny fingers stretched against the sky.

Last night the sky filled with geese
those voices high and strange
and far away who cried: Good-bye!

The next day: forty degrees and raining.
The earth shivers in its cloudy robe.
Crows swarm and go.

Today, in the wind: a tremolo:
weasel and snowshoe hare
are slowly turning white.
Reflections before the fact.

NOVEMBER AGAIN

Gray. Dark. Return. Chimney smoke lies down
crawls across the meadow like a slow soft snake.

Done. His woodshed full of wood, his little house banked tight
against the cold, the cellar full of meat and vegetables,
he comes inside
and washes blood and summer from his fingernails. In silence now
in the dying year he darkens like the days; he sits and falls,
as leaves fell, deeper into the coming dark, into the time of dream.

Quiet. Quiet. Still.
In the darkening afternoon
watching stove light flicker.

This is the end. The earth is empty again.

The long night steps slowly over the mountains.
The sky steals light from both ends of the day.

PART II

JOURNEY FOR THE NORTH

First, the first white man
ever to arrive and settle in this place speaks,
this man—restless and discontented with where he had been,
wanting
the fulfillment of a vision of what might be.
Then another man speaks,
he who came here for the same reasons 180 years later.

✦

I left my home in southern Connecticut late in January of 1789 and with
   my wife and two children,
both of whom were girls, the eldest being ten,
I started on my journey for the north
with a team of oxen and one horse, a sledge, and what provisions I had
   deemed necessary for such an undertaking.
About one hundred miles short of our destination one of my oxen failed.
A few days later the horse failed also, and after that I spent most of every
   day in the yoke next to our one remaining animal
and my wife and children walked behind or pushed as was necessary.

✦

North . . .
to ancient, rounded mountains
all ledge and rock outcropping
yet softened green by forest,
maple, beech, birch, ash and poplar,
larch, spruce, hemlock, cedar, pine
and fir—pointing toward the sky.

✦

We reached a settlement, now known as Johnson, some twenty-four miles
   west of our final destination toward the end of March
nearly starven and without the horse or ox.

I had left the downed animals with settlers in the areas where they fell
with the firm, if vain, hope of returning for them in the spring.

Although I had left Connecticut with numerous tools,
it had been necessary along the way to trade them for the provisions that
we needed.
When we arrived at our place of residence where we intended to make a
settlement,
I had only one axe and an old hoe with which to begin clearing land and
growing crops.
That first summer I cleared about two acres with only an axe, my one
remaining ox being too sick to be of any help at that time.

✦

Mountains and hill farms, valleys and bottomland
and in the bottom, always, water—
a river or a stream,
white and rocky, slow and muddy,
and in the bottom also, always, villages, because—
gristmill, sawmill, creamery—
power, log course, sewer.

Now, half of what they were a hundred years ago,
but still inhabited
by the beast who sleeps at night and walks upright,
in a landscape overwhelmed still
by something other than
what we have made,
by mountains and valleys,
water and sky, open land
and trees.

At the time of our settlement this was a wilderness and not the place of habitation it is now.
To the east it was thirty miles to the nearest human beings, and no road but marked trees;
to the south, also about thirty miles to the nearest infant settlement, but there was no communication with us,
and to the north, the woods stretched indefinite, to and beyond the border with Canada.

✦

One village of the many—call it Judevine.
Thirty-six square miles, a billion, billion souls,
six hundred human souls,
two-thirds in the mountains, two hundred in the village,
squeezed between sharp-rising hills,
room only for the highway, railroad, river
and what houses could be put
amongst the three.

And through the valley flows
the river.

✦

In those early days we were burdened with such a scarce sufficiency as to barely support our natures
and our only respite from continual hunger was what the river gave us.
Often during a day of clearing land, late in the forenoon, I would faint from hunger, whereupon, when I awoke,
I would take a fish by angling from the river, broil it on the riverbank, and then commence work again.
Toward evening I would again take enough fish by angling for myself and my family to provide us with that day's only sustenance.
We ate these gifts of the river without salt or bread, as we had neither salt nor flour at that time.

By the end of our first year in Judevine I had acquired an additional ox by
    laboring in the fields of other men, and we were able
in our second year to plant and harvest enough corn to provide ourselves
    meal for the entire winter.

✦

For a million years
the river raced and languished through this valley
and there were no human souls to see it.
(I wish I'd seen it then.)
Only water and trees and beasts of forest and stream.

Later, Indians, resident here for millennia, a people
and a way of life we know nothing of. And before them . . .
who?

In 1789 we arrived, because . . .
Greed or the desire to be alone, or more likely the yearning
for no constraints, license to do what you will, freedom
from law, society, the obligation to anything but the self—
the wonder and the flaw in our collective personality.

Or was it the dream of the hidden, inner, mystic life
growing in a wilderness, alone, where
inward and outward, other and self, disappear
and the spirit of wholeness rises
definite and sweet as dawn?

✦

Though I was doomed to encounter many additional perils, to suffer
    fatigue and toil on into the future,
our lives began to improve in both character and aspect,
and it seemed to me at that time the Divine Benefactor began rewarding
    me for my labor and my diligence.

The reader will be able to discern an example of His Good Providence in
  the incident which happened to me one late winter day
as I was proceeding home from the mill with my team and a load of meal.

✦

<u>This never-ending dream</u>
<u>of freedom and bread.</u>

✦

I approached the river at a location where I had often crossed before, but,
being ignorant then of the devious and dangerous nature of the river and
  its ice at this time of the year,
I drove my oxen onto the river. When about half across, I perceived the ice
  settling under my animals.
I jumped onto the tongue of my sled and hastened to the oxen's heads and
  pulled out the pin that held the yoke.
By this time the oxen were sunk to their knees in water.
I then sprang to the sled and drawed it back to the shore without the least
  difficulty, notwithstanding the load, and returned to my oxen.

✦

I mean, in 1789 we *began* to arrive.
Not a steady stream, but waves—
like all migrations, conquerings, people driven from a place
by dissatisfactions, persecutions, restlessness, pulled toward
some other place by dream.

✦

By this time they had broken a considerable path in the ice and were
  struggling to get out.
I could do nothing but stand and see them swim round.
Sometimes they would be nearly out of sight, nothing scarcely but their
  horns to be seen;
they would then rise and struggle to extricate themselves from their perilous
  situation.

At length the oxen swam up to where I stood and laid their heads on the
   ice at my feet.
I immediately took the yoke from off their necks; they lay still till the act
   was performed
and then returned to swimming as before.

✦

First Anglo stock—English, Scot,
from the colonies to the south, mostly from Connecticut:
Stanton, Mead, Middlebrooks, Taylor, Lane, Sedgwick, Bacon,
Pettibone, Fairchilds, Kingsbury, Herrick, Crocker, Pixley, Shed.

And very shortly after, from the north,
maybe for the same reasons, the French came,
down across the border from Quebec:
Bourdeau, La Casse, La Croix, Ladeau, Larocque, Lavoie,
Le Blanc, Leroux, Levèsque, Poulin, Deschamps, Tétreault,
Desjardins, Devereaux, Patenaud, St. George, St. Jacques,
Turcotte, LaMotte, Bassette and Gelineau.

Again, later in the century, Italians, Spaniards, Greeks,
stonecutters come to work the quarries:
Scrizzi, Faziano, Albrizio, Tortellini, Gomez, Echeveria,
Rublacabla.

✦

By this time they had made an opening in the ice as much as two rods
   across.
One of them finally swam to the downstream side, and in an instant, as if
   lifted out of the water,
he was on his side on the ice, and got up and walked off;
the other swam to the same place and was out in the same manner.

I stood on the opposite side of the opening and saw with astonishment
   every movement.
I then thought, and the impression is still on my mind, that they were
   helped out by supernatural means; most certainly

no natural cause could produce an effect such as this;
that a heavy ox six and a half feet in girth, can of his own natural
strength heave himself out of the water on his side on the ice.

◆

Then again, toward the end of the 1960s, another wave of young,
out of suburbs and cities and into these hills:
Hewitt, Landi, Klein, Liberman, Solomon, Plent.
Hippies.
Katzenberg, Bernstein, Coe.
Goddamned hippies!
All, pulled toward this place by dream.

◆

So who's native?
Don't talk to me native.
Because you got here early
makes you more?

Witch grass, zucchini, tomatoes,
you and me—
all immigrants is what I'm talking.
Native is dirt and stones, mountains.
What else?

We, love, are water
Oi!
just passing through.

◆

That in the course of Divine Providence events take place
out of the common course of nature that our strongest reasoning cannot
*   comprehend is impious to deny.*
Others have a right to doubt my testimony, but in this instance, for me to
*   doubt would be perjury to my own conscience*
and ingratitude to my Divine Benefactor.

◆

Then in the 1970s yet another immigrant: coyote,
from the Dakotas, or Minnesota maybe, north to Canada
and east, where they mixed with timber wolves,
grew bigger, bushier, became "the new wolf,"
then dropped down again across the border.
Now their song is also added to this place.

It is fitting that this hybrid scavenger—want to call him bas-
tard?—
should join us here, take up with us other illegitimates. Purity?
Source of madness, retardation, bane of Spanish kings.
Give me instead Thucydides Augustus McInnes
(he's known as Cyd).
Scot, Irish, Italian, who knows what else? Product of our mixing;
a foil, once, as we are now, to this hillbound, inbred, narrow
insularity. Some might call it madness. (I might call it that.)
Yet here we are, another wave, flowing toward tomorrow,
hybrids, immigrants, bastards: which is the way it's always been.

◆

When I reflect on past events, the fatigue and toil I had to endure, the
    dark scenes I had to pass through,
I am struck with wonder and astonishment at the fortitude and presence
    of mind that I had then to bear me up under them.
I exercised all my powers to the best I could, and left the effect for future
    events to decide, without embarrassing my mind with imaginary evils.
I could lie down at night, forgetting my troubles and sleep composed and
    calm as a child.
I did, in reality, experience the just proverb of the wise man,
that the sleep of the laboring man is sweet,
whether he eat little or much.

◆

Drawn toward this place by dream, we,
like those who came before, for reasons we can't speak,
take root, become this place, define it.

We are here and always leaving.
We are water, like the river,
just passing through.

✦

Nor can I close my tale of sufferings without rendering my feeble tribute of
thanks and praise to my Benign Benefactor,
who supplies the wants of the needy and relieves the distressed, and who,
in His Providential Kindness has assisted my natural strength, both of
body and mind, to endure those scenes of distress and toil.

✦

Providential Kindness, bless us,
and bless night-singing coyote.
Bless all souls alive in Judevine,
and bless the ghosts.

Give us Benediction.

✦ ✦ ✦

ROY MCINNES

I

Roy McInnes is a welder. He spends his life
with chains and block and tackle, steel and torches,
lives his days inside a hood looking like
a medieval warrior, peering through a small rectangle
of blackened glass, watching light brighter than the sun.
He listens to the groan of generators, the crack and snap
of an electric arc liquifying steel.
His hands are always dark and on his upper lip
is a mustache
as if wiped there by a greasy finger.

Roy McInnes is a small man and frail.
He speaks quietly and slowly and moves that way.
He seems at ease inside his body, comfortable there.
When you shake his hand his grip is warm and gentle
and you can feel the calm he carries in his person
flow into your arm.

Roy and I were visiting one day, years ago,
after we had got to know each other some,
and we got to talking about work
and I said, because I was afraid to tell the truth,
that I'd just about rather garden than do anything,
to which Roy responded, and there seemed to be
some sadness in his voice:
Well, I don't know about just about.
All I know is what I'd rather do than anything.
I'd rather weld.

Roy's truck is an extension of himself,
which is not to be confused with the way some people
buy a fancy car with velour seats, electric windows
and suddenly start wearing cardigans and oxfords,
suddenly become
little more than yet another piece of optional equipment.
In Roy's life it is the truck that gets transformed.

I met his truck the day I first met him.
Not that he introduced me or anything like that,
it's just you can't help noticing.

When Roy bought the truck new-to-him, it was just a pickup,
a common insect like a million others identical to it.
He brought it home, put it in his shop and six weeks later
it emerged a strange, metallic butterfly, unique and fanciful,
translated to
an articulation of his private vision,
a function of Roy's need and whimsy.

New, the truck was rated at three-quarter ton,
but with the added braces to the frame, heavier shocks,
special springs, dual rear wheels and heavy duty tires
it can carry four.

Roy cut the bed away right down to the frame
and welded on a diamond-plate floor and roof,
using two inch steel pipe for posts, one at each corner,
one in the middle on each side. Then up forward,
toward the cab and halfway back, he welded
sheet-metal walls and welded shelves to them
and all the shelves have doors on hinges, all made of steel.
There are hooks and clamps welded to the walls everywhere

so when he goes down a bumpy road his tools won't bounce
  around.

Roy McInnes is a carpenter who builds with steel,
with boilerplate and torches.
In place of nails he binds his dream
with hydrogen and oxyacetylene.

Shaper, molder, alchemist,
intermediary, priest,
his hands communicate a vision,
they create with skill and grace
an act of intercession between reality and need.

III

Roy's house and shop are on the edge of town.
The shop was built in stages.
The tall center section with its steep-pitched roof
is sided with slabs from the local mill, whereas
the lean-to shed on the left
is particleboard; the one on the right is Homasote.

Summer people say it's ugly, but what they can't, or won't,
understand is: the sidings write a history
of its construction. Rome wasn't built in a day either.

When Roy built the center section he needed an opening
large enough to admit big trucks, like loggers' rigs,
but couldn't afford the kind of rising, jointed,
overhead doors gas stations and garages have,
so he found a way to use salvaged storm doors,
the kind with glass so he could get some light in there,
by hitching them with hinges side to side
and stacking them three high so that now he's got

two folding doors which make an opening fifteen feet wide
and seventeen feet high: two doors of doors
made from eighteen smaller doors.

Roy heats the shop with a homemade, quadruple-chamber,
oil-drum stove: four fifty-five gallon drums:
two side by side above one, the firebox, and one above the two:
a glowing diamond of cylinders all welded to each other
and held apart by rods and all connected by a pipe
which leads the smoke from one drum to another and finally,
when it has bled the smoke of heat, exits to the chimney.

Beyond the stove at the back of the shop
stacked willy-nilly against the wall
there is an intricate confusion of iron pipes, cast iron scraps,
angle iron, sheets of aluminum and steel, diamond plate,
expanded metal, loops of heavy wire and braided cable
and a half-dozen categories of other things I can't identify—
a mine, the raw material of his dreams.

The shop is always cluttered, dirty, and there is
a permanent grime that clings to everything.
Generators and tanks of gas, and orange rubber hoses
snaked across the floor. The place smells of oil and grease,
of that molecular rearrangement of the air the welder's arc
produces.

This is a place where—against the grinder's scream and whine,
the moan of generators straining, the crackling spit of metal
rent asunder—human speech is pointless, drowned
in a cacophony of unearthly voices. And when the machines
get still, it is a place to see through the smoky fog
something medieval, brooding, dark, fantastical.

It would be so easy to see this place as sinister,

to see the wizard-priest who rules this lair as evil,
that would be so easy if
you didn't know that he is Roy—
the one who lets the calm of his body flow into your arm
when you touch his hand.

IV

Stand in the highway; look at the shop straight on;
pretend it isn't what it is; get beyond its function.
Look at its lines, at the proportions of height to width,
sheds to center section—an early Christian basilica,
or something Gothic.

The tall center section, narrow, steep-roofed—the nave.
The sheds—the aisles,
roofed-over flying buttresses.
And those doors of doors are cathedral doors.
There are no rose windows here, no clerestory, no triforium,
no vaulted ceilings or clustered piers, and it's ratty,
but it soars—not too high or very gracefully,
but it soars.

It is a January day.
The doors of doors fold open.
Roy appears in hood and grimy apron.

Then, just down the road, smoking through the village,
the penitent comes, the one who seeks the healing touch
of fire.

Guy Desjardins, trucker of logs and lumber,
who just this morning while loading the biggest butt-log beech
he ever saw in his life, snapped the boom.
The truck lurches down the road, clam and boom dangling,
a wounded beast, Gargantua's broken arm. Guy shifts down,

pulls to the doors of doors and in.

There are no acolytes, no choir,
but the engine sings its cracked and pulsing song
and the censer spurts heady clouds of smoke to the rafters.

The doors come closed, truck shuts down
and for a moment Guy and Roy stand
before the diamond juggernaut of cylinders, their hands
outstretched in ritualistic adulation, a prelude to the mass.
The boom is jacked and steadied, readied for the altar
of cutting flame: The Mass of Steel and Fire.

From the clutter of his accidental reredos
Roy brings angle iron. A ball-peen hammer bangs,
generator moans, light arcs and snaps, steel flows
a second time—a liquid balm, metallic salve
and the healing touch.

When the clanging mass is finished, when the groans
and snaps and spits have ceased, when there is silence,
when only a spirituous wisp of greasy smoke ascends
toward the blue-foggy rafters, when Guy stands
knowing it is done, the celebrant lifts his hood
and says benediction:
That ought to hold it, Guy.

They drink coffee from dirty cups,
eat doughnuts with greasy hands.
Then Guy backs out, is gone, smoking down the road,
back to the job, leaning on his horn and waving
in what has got to be plainsong, a canticle,
praise and joy for the man,
a chorus of hallelujahs, for
the reconciling arc of fire.

CYD

Thucydides Augustus McInnes went into the woods when he
   was twelve and spent his life logging with horses
and only at the age of eighty did he begin spending his winters in
   the welding shop with Roy, his son.

Yet even then he spent summers in the mountains, compromising
only in his last years by logging with a team of ponies because:
It got so I couldn't give the horses all the work they wanted.
I embarrassed them. These ponies here do less . . . like me.
We're suited to each other.

Thucydides Augustus McInnes was a logger for so long that there
are mountainsides around here he logged twice in his one lifetime.

When you met him, he did not reach out and shake your hand
as does his son, but rather he remained within himself
and bent his upper body forward, shyly. He almost bowed.

Thucydides Augustus McInnes was not a talker.
He could sit quietly not saying anything and visit—be—with you
and neither you nor he would be embarrassed.
It always seemed to me
he was a reincarnation of Lao Tzu.

Yet, lest you think him ephemeral or unearthly, he could dance,
even at the age of eighty, a clogging dance
with an authenticity, a verve and grace
no one who learns it for nostalgia's sake can ever muster.

The winter my wife carried our daughter in her womb,
Cyd came up with his ponies and his dray to help us draw our
   wood. I have a picture somewhere.
We are in the dooryard, at the woodshed door.

Snow is everywhere. We have just unloaded and have paused—
before we head back to the woods—
long enough for me to take the picture.
The ponies are waiting and steaming. My wife—my daughter
bulging beneath her coat—and Cyd stand on the empty dray.
Both of them are smiling. Cyd's cheek bulges with his plug,
you can see his stained tobacco teeth.
His eyes are warm and drenching—
alive as the sunlight on the first real day of spring.
His eyes are filled with his delight at being in the presence of this
beautiful and young woman who is carrying a child.

Thucydides Augustus McInnes, who was known as Cyd, and
    nobody's fool,
loved his horses and cared for them as well as any man. But—
and I must tell you this, because you should not get the wrong
    impression of this man, you should not think him soft—
I have seen him take his peavey and strike a horse on the hock
above a rear hoof and shout in fury at the beast until
the animal regained its understanding
of who it was gave the directions.

At the age of seventy-nine, Cyd went to Florida intending
to spend two weeks visiting with friends, but left two days
after his arrival and came home. When I saw him
down at The Garage and asked him how his trip had been,
he said: Well, sir, that place I was, that condominium,
had rules to keep out
all the animals and children.
Can you imagine that?
How could anybody spend his life without animals and children?

Thucydides Augustus McInnes died three days ago
and today was buried
up near the top of the sidehill cemetery just east of town,
the one that looks down—across the valley and the river,

the one that looks out—toward a mountainside
Thucydides Augustus McInnes
logged twice in his one lifetime.

SALLY TATRO'S PLACE

Even now, years after its desertion, and though it is
gray and sinking and its parts come apart, the house
still clings to a former grace—narrow clapboards,
fluted corners, a center door with frosted glass—
and, in addition to dishevelment, dilapidation,
the place suffers weeds high as the windows,
a porch roof fallen in, though it now
fades and weathers, slips irretrievably away,

when I drive past I watch and think how it is like
old poetry where reference and allusion are obscure
but where, even after centuries, insight and need
still swell within the form, and I see in the

collapsing house the builder's passion rising
from design: this indestructible, eternal dream.

ENVOY TO SALLY'S PLACE

There was a fellow passing through who lived and worked
in New York City, an official of some sort down there at the
Metropolitan Museum of Art is what I heard.
He was summering up here, I think, and going down the road
when he spied Sally's place and was so stunned
by its beauty and its calm, so taken aback by finding

such a work of art so far from anywhere,
he drove his car right off the road.

When Roy saw what happened he came running
figuring the fellow must be hurt, but before Roy could get
to where the car tilted in the ditch the fellow climbed out,
walked nonchalantly across the road
and began taking pictures of the house.

Roy comes up to him out of breath and says:
You okay?

And the gent turns around surprised and says:
Huh? Oh. Yes. Fine. Thank you.
and then says:
Does anybody here know how beautiful this place is?
Oh!

Roy didn't say much but did pull the fellow out
and he was on his way.

When Edith heard the story her mouth tightened as it does
when she gets mad and she said:
Yes, we know, or used to know.
It *was* a lovely place, but not now, not anymore.
What's beautiful about an empty house?
It's falling down, deserted, cold inside,
what's beautiful about that?

You should have seen that place when the Tatros
still were there, when there was flowers in the dooryard
and the barn wasn't falling down, paint on the clapboards
and wash on the line and the pastures clear because of cows—
then it was beautiful. Now it's just a wreck,
a picture for that fellow's old museum.

BEAUDRY'S LAWN SALE

A low-slung sagging house
those red-gray asphalt shingles
made to look like bricks
and the sheds of weathered wood
sagging too. All the roofs drooping.
Surrounded by ranks of gutted cars
and out front in the space
between the house and road
where there might have been
a lawn—a lawn sale instead.

Worn Formica kitchen tables,
the chrome legs blistering.
Coke and beer bottles, stacks
of plates and saucers (no two
alike), cups without handles,
electric motors that may
but probably won't work, one
overstuffed chair, six
television sets, old clothing,
innumerable knick-knacks and
everything covered with sheets
of plastic held down by rocks—
everything guaranteed dry.

This is a permanent sale.
Summer and winter it is here
which is why there is grass growing
in a cereal bowl or two.

If you are on the trail of an
antique, don't stop here—please.
This is not nostalgia's place.

No hidden gems resting unrecognized
amid the clutter. These people
know the worth of things
better than you think.

Here
are only bits and pieces
of a way of life,
these artifacts for sale:
the shards of want.

ELEGY FOR CHARLIE KETTER

I

Across the road from Beaudry's
was Charlie Ketter's—the nicest place in town.
His house and yard were always spic-and-span,
neat as a pin, and they therefore stood out
as a cared-for oasis
in the general rubble of the village.
He had a lawn, and the lawn was spread
with the wishing wells and birdhouses he made
and sold. His wishing wells were red and white
and blue and the birdhouses came in shapes
of sugarhouses, only you could never tell
which ones were for sale since he had a lot
of favorites that he never sold.

II

There was one thing odd about Charlie Ketter.
He was a Democrat, one of three in thirty-six
square miles. I heard a dozen people say:

I just can't understand that Charlie Ketter.
He's the nicest man what ever trod in shoes,
and he's a Democrat!

III

Charlie died two years ago
at the age of forty-three
of a cancer that daily
in the last year of his life
marched through his body
like hardhack and weed trees
filling in an unattended field.

IV

Now Charlie's wife is gone,
moved on to somewhere smaller,
and the Ketter place begins its turn
from order to decline, its fall
toward weeds and boards collapsed
upon themselves, a confusion
like a cancer
within the human frame.

JERRY'S GARAGE

In Craftsbury there are two: Raboin's and Humphrey's;
down in New Hampshire, in West Andover,
it is Thornley's;
in Five Islands, Maine,
it's called Grover's;
and between Lake Champlain
and the Atlantic Ocean there has got to be

a thousand known only as The Corner Store.

Almost all have gas pumps, only some
have mechanics or a post office
and I'd wager none
still have all three.

Here in Judevine we call it The Garage
or Jerry's.

Jerry's is
and is in
the center of the town.
It's not a place that used to be something else
and got converted to its present use. It's always been
a place for food and vehicles. First as a store and stable
and a wheelwright's shop, then, with cars, a store and gas pumps,
a mechanic and a lift. A place, since it began, to serve
two of the very few necessities: food and transportation.

The place that serves necessities becomes one;
which means, when there is nothing else to do,
when you are lonely, you go to The Garage
and stand around, or sit, and visit.

Conrad works at the garage because he may as well,
if he didn't have a job there he'd be there anyway,
which is why he got hired in the first place.
As Jerry smiling says: Hell,
if he's gonna be here all the time, he might as well
be doin' somethin'.

Conrad smirks and says: An' git paid.

Like all places of its kind

it's got a little bit of some things and not much of anything:
milk, eggs, lousy bread, tobacco—both to smoke and chew—
ammunition, candy, a smattering of canned goods,
toilet paper, a little dog food, one can of Similac,
fishing tackle, pickled eggs, produce when the season's right,
motor oil, the local papers, magazines,
maybe a book or two by a local writer, a little hardware,
and wine, shelves and shelves of wine and even more beer,
at least a couple coolers full—hundreds of cases
of beer.

For years Jerry talked about how he'd like to have
a restaurant hitched to the store—
there was an empty room out back would do.
It'd make it nice, he'd say, to have a place
to take a bowl of soup, a sandwich,
a place to sit and visit.
He talked that way for years,
then just a couple months ago
his dream got muscled out by deed
and Jerry's got himself a restaurant now—
a Judevine-type restaurant—
in the back room, the counter faced
in three different kinds of paneling,
a meat slicer he picked up at auction,
a hot plate from Alice's junk store and two
Formica kitchen tables and some chairs
with plastic seats from Beaudry's perennial lawn sale.

They make grinders, a different soup each day,
five days a week, and you can buy a soda in the store
to drink with lunch—but no beer,
unless you drink it outside,
the license costs too much.

Well, it ain't much. Jerry says:

Got some beat-up equipment, nailed together scraps.
(He's an ecologist, you see?)
Just like everything else in Judevine: half-assed.

Which it is and seedy too,
but such aesthetic judgments depend on point of view.
From where I look I see
something good enough for us or anybody:
a place to sit down, visit, eat and drink together,
even if it is a grinder and a Pepsi,
a place to let our caring for each other grow, which,
as everybody knows, has nothing at all to do
with soft lights and leather booths.

NEED, NECESSITY, DELIGHT,
OR,
A WASHING MACHINE FOR A FLOWERPOT

Every summer morning at fifteen minutes to seven
Jerry descends the stairs from his apartment above The Garage,
unlocks the store, turns off the nighttime lights,
turns on the gas pumps and the air compressor,
then moves to the lunchroom, plugs in the coffeepot
and, while he waits for his morning coffee,
he goes outside and wheels an ancient washing machine,
the kind that is a tub on legs, the legs on casters,
the wringer and the agitator long since gone,
away from the side of the building
and out to one end of the gas pumps.

The washing machine is full of dirt
and in the dirt grow giant orange and yellow marigolds.
He pinches off what blossoms may be dying, any withered leaves,
does the necessary weeding, and then, if they need it,

waters them with the battered, galvanized can
he uses to fill radiators.

In Jerry's old washing machine metaphored to flowerpot
I see the whole history of what I know of human art and thought.
Thales and Anaximander, thinking, trying to find that one thing
out of which all else comes, Pythagoras, slowly or
KA-BLAM! (as in Archimedes in the tub) when he discovers
a universal truth about certain kinds of triangles,
Anselm and Abelard as they debate the function of our words,
Hegel and the process of our thought,
or Einstein, fingers to his lower lip, dreaming
on the nature of time and space and energy.

Is it ridiculous to compare Jerry's flowerpot
to Einstein or Hegel, Abelard or Pythagoras?
They all took the old, the given, the known
and found in it something new,
that satisfying, exciting, delightful leap
of human sense and mind
from known to unknown.
Whether it is a washing machine for a flowerpot,
a pickup truck transmogrified to a specific need
or a poem
in which a ramshackled, tumbledown ratty pile of boards
known as a welding shop becomes a Gothic hymn to God,
it is the making of a metaphor, a bridge, that leap
from known to unknown.

To see the thing not for what it is or is thought to be
but for what it could be
because you must and must because
you are driven to delight by necessity, by need—
is imagination.

Some people look at Judevine and only see decay
because they don't remember necessity *or* need.
The words are lost somewhere inside them, pickled
in the sauce of affluence, atrophied by the tenure of security.
They don't remember that the decay they see is need
and need is the ground in which necessity
gives birth to the imagination.

When necessity gets pickled her child packs up and leaves,
goes some place else where she can find her mother.
Judevine is such a place.
Imagination lives here because her mamma lives here too.

In the midst of what some think is squalor,
necessity and the imagination yield delight—
like Roy's truck and shop, or Jerry's flowerpot,
these metaphors,
for the eternal, elemental searching of the human soul—
and they bloom,
because this ground is rich with need.

BEN

You can see him in the village almost anytime.
He's always on the street.
At noon he ambles down to Jerry's
in case a trucker who's stopped by for lunch
might feel like buying him a sandwich.
Don't misunderstand, Ben's not starving;
he's there each noon because he's sociable,
not because he's hungry.
He is a friend to everyone except the haughty.

There are at least half a dozen families in the village

who make sure he always has enough to eat
and there are places
where he's welcome to come in and spend the night.

Ben is a cynic in the Greek and philosophic sense,
one who gives his life to simplicity
seeking only the necessities
so he can spend his days
in the presence of his dreams.

Ben is a vision of another way,
the vessel in this place for
ancient Christian mystic, Buddhist recluse, Taoist hermit.
Chuang Tzu, The Abbot Moses, Meister Eckhart,
Khamtul Rimpoche, Thomas Merton—
all these and all the others live in Ben, because

in America only a dog
can spend his days
on the street or by the river
in quiet contemplation
and be fed.

CONRAD

Conrad. Forty-three.
Works at The Garage
rents a room from Flossie
just next door
has his separate entrance so
everything will be
on the up-and-up.

Changes tires, takes the bottles
but never works the register.

What do I owe you, Conrad?
Well . . . you . . . I don't know.
You better go ask Jerry.

Every evening when the valley darkens
just about the time
the lights go on above the gas pumps,
Conrad begins. Beer
and blackberry brandy.
By closing time at eight
he hovers in the low and darkened room
like a dazed cat.

Jerry locks up, puts out the lights,
except for the one in the window that says:

Beer

and Conrad pads the hundred feet to home
tilting between
broken cars and snow machines,
headed for his separate entrance.

Supper? Huh?

The beer is filling.
Think of all those calories.
The sugar in the brandy
gives him carbohydrates.
His protein comes from television.
He dines each night in black and white.
He builds his bone and muscle from
a two-dimensional dream.

Now he is rugged, handsome, swift and mean.
There is a gorgeous woman hanging on his sleeve.

Conrad's only failure is as a novelist.
He never learned to lie. Don't pity him.
Pity yourself instead. Ask if you have more
or whether it is simply, as it is with me,
that you write better fiction for your life.

JERRY WILLEY'S LUNCH

Before Jerry got The Garage he worked for the Mountain
  Company down in Stowe
helping New York ladies off the lifts,
all day on top the mountain freezing his ass off
for two and a quarter an hour.
Jerry never brought a lunch, not once in all those years,
just six pieces of bread, a jar of mayonnaise and a soda which
each morning when he reached the mountain top he placed
inside the warming hut beside the skiers' lunches
left there so they wouldn't freeze.

As Jerry said: I ain't eatin' salt pork and macaroni
when I got these. Then he'd unwrap half a dozen
skiers' sandwiches, extract a slice or two from each—
roast beef, corned beef, ham, pastrami—
rewrap them carefully and fix his lunch.